THINK & WIN BIG

ALSO BY SKIP J. WILLIAMS

Think Progress

SKIP J. WILLIAMS

THINK & WIN BIG

75 QUICK & POWERFUL SECRETS FOR PERSONAL SUCCESS

PIKS BOOKS

Piks Books, a division of Skip Williams Communications LLC, New York

Piks Books may be ordered via booksellers and purchased in bulk for educational, business, fund-raising, or sales promotional use. For information, please e-mail piksinfo@skipwilliamsonline.com

Think & Win Big: 75 Quick & Powerful Secrets For Personal Success
ISBN 978-0-9839818-0-0 (2012 edition / Paperback)
ISBN 978-0-9839818-1-7 (2012 edition / eBook)

Printed in the United States of America

Second Edition

*To All The Winners Worldwide and
The Skip Williams All-Star Team*

CONTENTS

TODAY'S MASTERPIECE

What did you do toward your dreams today?

Every day is a brand new day, which means "today" is a brand new starting point for you to succeed. Whatever happened yesterday is past tense today. When your goals, objectives, and purpose are to succeed, you don't have time to dwell on what happened yesterday. Thinking back on yesterday, last week, last year, or ten years ago will keep you from moving forward today. In order for you to be victorious, you will need to place your focus and actions on what you will accomplish *today*.

In his book, *Think Like A Champion*, the real estate mogul Donald Trump stated, "If you see every day as an important day for your future and a special day just because you have it, you will be amazed at how productive and energetic you will be." Every morning, upon waking up I say, "Hello world!" This creates a positive energy for me to have a productive day. Recently, a friend asked me, do I ever have *bad* days? I replied, "Yes, I do have bad days." Then, she inquired, "So, what do you do when you have bad days?" With a smile on my face, I said, "When I have bad days, I don't view them as a problem. I view them as a *challenge*. Problems will depress you. Challenges excite me. Also, it's the challenges that make my day and life super exciting."

As human beings, we are challenged every second of our lives. Within every *challenge*, we never know exactly what will happen or what life will present us with – good or bad. Challenges are a part of life and you can overcome them. It will be your *challenges* that will show you how to succeed. It will be your *challenges* that will push you forward when your mind is contemplating on giving up. It will be your *challenges* that will lead you to new opportunities.

> *"Every day life places a brand new canvas
> in front of you, so you can design your
> own masterpiece."*

John C. Maxwell, author and leadership expert asserted in *Make Today Count*, "Nobody says that good decisions are always simple, but they are necessary for success." The starting line to every result you produce begins with the decisions and actions that you make within every moment of your life. From the moment you wake up, until the moment you go to sleep, you are in charge of your own individual paintbrush to how you want your life to look. Every day life places a brand new canvas in front of you, so you can design your own masterpiece. Today is your day! What masterpiece will you paint today? Which mixture of colors will you choose today? How will you showcase your creativity today?

As the originator of your life, you can create your own vivid outcome with your own creativity. It's been said, "We see what we want to see." What are you looking at in your life? Do you see yourself succeeding or failing? Are you visualizing yourself winning or losing? Do you envision yourself enthusiastic or depressed? Do you imagine yourself creating a better life for yourself, or do you picture yourself staying complacent and complaining about your life?

What did you do toward your dreams today? The previous question was the exact inquiry that not only woke up my mind and creativity–it also ignited my passion and determination to succeed. Every day this question pushes me to excel because it continues to remind me to think bigger and aim higher. There is one key distinction that all winners have in common: Winners are always looking at the bigger picture. In spite of the obstacles and challenges in front of them, winners always envision themselves winning. You are a winner! As a winner, you must be willing to think bigger and aim higher. You are the architect of your own dreams–strive to make every day your masterpiece. What masterpiece will you create today?

2

THINK CREATIVE

If the world depended on your creativity,
how creative would you be?

Richard Carlson, author of *Don't Worry, Make Money*, wrote, "Successful people know that the one aspect of life that they do have control over is their own thinking. All of us have this same advantage, so let's all start there." Have you ever asked yourself, "What are successful people doing that I'm not doing?" The answer is simple. Successful people have learned how to mentally activate their own creative thinking.

Thinking creative is the starting line to making successful things happen. Every success starts with a creative mindset. Fashion designers, entertainers, entrepreneurs, authors, and architects are renowned for their creativity. Creative thinkers are visionary leaders. Winners are creative thinkers because they are constantly seeking new ways to display their own ideas. Rather than following the status quo, winners go beyond what others fail to see. For example, instead of looking at the green grass only on *one* side of the fence, creative thinkers look for opportunities to make their grass grow greener on *both* sides of the fence.

Steve Jobs, the founder, CEO and Chairman of Apple, made the Apple brand a household name, due to his creative intelligence. Steve Jobs' vision for Apple has been phenomenal. The Apple computers, iPods, iPhones, and iPads have not only changed the technology industry, they have changed the vision of how we think, produce, and succeed. The creativity of Steve Jobs has made the Apple brand legendary. Creativity is everywhere. If you have a mobile phone, you're holding creativity in your hand. If you have an iPhone or Smartphone, you will see the creativity via the numerous applications (known as "apps") that are available for you to download. Every day more creative thinkers are discovering innovative ways to make a difference in the world by developing various types of apps. If you need to find something, I'm sure there's an app for it.

Winners know success begins with a dream or an idea, which starts in the mind. As a winner, it will be your own creativity that will produce your own success. If you have an idea, and it's been sitting on your mental shelf for a long period of time, it may be time for you to pull it down off your mental shelf, blow the dust off of it, and take action toward it. Don't be afraid to be looked at or called an "outcast thinker." In other words, don't be afraid to think differently. One of the main reasons most people don't succeed in life is because they are afraid to think in a different way. Countless people think "inside" of the box, instead of thinking "outside" and "beyond" the box. As human beings, we are equipped with our own unique minds. Some of us have forgotten that we have our own minds.

Having your own mind means you can mentally choose how you want to think. With your own mind, you can mentally visualize and design your own success. Do you recall, as a kid growing up, how you saw someone doing something then you said, "That's what I want to do" or "That's what I would like to be when I grow up?" That was your introduction to creative thinking. Your *vision* of success starts in your own mind. Your *results* of success start within your own actions.

As a winner, you must be willing to open your mind, so you can think bigger. Having an open-mind is the platform for thinking big. Allowing your mind to absorb new concepts will enable you to grow to new heights and produce new results. Moreover, thinking bigger will give you the opportunity to literally see, create, and enjoy your own success.

The people who are willing to think creatively and take physical action toward their creative thoughts constantly stand out as winners. It's the creative thinkers who win and receive the opportunity to enjoy the best rewards in life. As a winner, open your mind to new opportunities. Whatever you want to *physically* achieve, you first must *mentally* achieve it. Put on your thinking cap. Start thinking creatively. Most importantly, start using your own creativity.

3

OUTSIDE YOUR COMFORT ZONE

Are you willing to grow uncomfortable?

Most people have designed their comfort zones, not just for "comfort," but also for their mental and emotional protection. It's as if our comfort zones have become our high walls of security without doors or windows to keep us away from the things that we fear. Some people are afraid to step outside of their comfort zones, because then they would have to face their fears, which many of them don't want to do. Are you "living" or "vacationing" in your comfort zone?

It's one thing to take a "vacation" in your comfort zone, because it will give you a moment to relax, and get your thoughts together. However, "living" in a comfort zone is like living inside of a comfortable *fear*. If you're *living* inside your comfort zone, when are you going to step outside of your comfort zone? Or should I ask, "When are you going to step outside of your *fear*? You can either live your life trapped inside your *fears*, or you can stand up and walk outside of them.

As human beings, we habitually develop comfort zones in our lives. Most of us have built our comfort zones around our habits. Many of our habits are good and productive, while some of our habits are bad and unproductive. Nonetheless, we let our habits grow into our comfort zones. When we limit ourselves inside our comfort zones, we keep ourselves from stretching our full potential. Why would you place limitations on yourself, when you have the opportunity to be limitless? What have you achieved *inside* of your comfort zone? Now ask yourself, "What could I achieve if I stepped *outside* of my comfort zone?"

Though introverts are known to reside inside of their comfort zones, at times they do extend themselves and go outside their realm. All of us can achieve more in our lives, once we take more steps outside of our own comfort zones. Who made your comfort zone for you? The answer is very obvious…YOU! You made your own comfort zone, which means you can either redesign it, stretch it, or breakthrough the comfort zones that you made for yourself. If you're not succeeding in your life, it may be time for you to step outside of your comfort zone.

Sometimes the best way to succeed is to become uncomfortable. One reason the majority of people don't succeed is because they have grown attached to their own comfort zones. They have become so comfortable inside of their own comfort zones that they refuse to leave them. For example, one afternoon, while I was talking with a gentleman, he told me that he didn't really like his job. The reason he hadn't left his job was because he had grown "comfortable" with it. This scenario happens on a daily basis. There are countless unhappy people who dread going to their jobs. Conversely, they continue to go anyway because they have grown comfortable with their jobs. Let me shake the beehive for a second. Let's say that you've grown comfortable with your job. One day you go to work and you receive a pink slip that states, "We no longer need your services," what would you do? How comfortable would you be after receiving the pink slip?

Always remember, life is to be learned, lived and enjoyed, not settled and wasted away. Why settle for <u>less</u>, when you can have <u>more</u> in your life? You can have more fun, happiness, wealth, and success in your life. It's never too late to start enjoying your own life. The best way to enjoy life is to literally start doing just that…enjoying it. Instead of sitting in the house, go outside. Rather than doing the same old same old, take up a new hobby, learn a new language, and do something more adventurous. Don't forget you're the designer who created your own comfort zone, which means you can give your comfort zone a makeover by stretching it to new territories.

As a winner, it's okay to go beyond your comfort zone. When it comes to expanding your comfort zone, there are over a billion options available to you. Begin challenging yourself every day to go beyond what you achieved yesterday. Learn more today. Achieve more today. Help more people today. When you go outside of your comfort zone, your triumphs will be endless.

4

THE MEANING OF OVERQUALIFIED

Is being overqualified a good or a bad thing in your book?

There are moments in our lives when we let our minds view certain things from the wrong side of the table. Have you ever noticed how some people will quickly get emotionally disturbed, or bent out of shape when someone tells them that they are "overqualified" for something?

A few weeks ago, I had a conversation with a young man named George, who had just left a job interview. George told me how he applied for various jobs, but this particular job interview disturbed him. After listening to George, I inquired, "How did the job interview go?" George replied, in a disgruntled tone, "They said I was *overqualified* for the position." Instead of looking at the comment from a "positive" angle, George instantly viewed it as a *negative* remark.

What happened to George occurs to numerous job hunters every day. When someone says, "You are overqualified" for something that is not a bad thing. In fact, *it's a plus*, not a minus. Also, you could view it as a *compliment*. Whenever people convey that you're overqualified, they are silently telling you, "You have more potential within you than what you're putting out."

"Many people will see the potential in you, even when you don't see the potential within yourself."

I am always seeking innovative people with great potential. When I see a person with potential, I give him or her the opportunity to display their talents. One reason I do this is because I enjoy surrounding myself with winners. Winners see the potential in other winners. Many people will see the potential *in* you, even when you don't see the potential *within* yourself. Some people will overlook your potential, but that's not a reason to catch an attitude or get upset. As a winner, it's always your responsibility to believe in yourself and in your own potential. As I stated to one of my clients, "Never let someone talk you out of maximizing your own potential."

Be "overqualified" if you may–but never enter a location *unqualified*. People will tell you that you're overqualified, but that doesn't mean you've failed. It's an indication that you have more to give. Don't minimize your potential. Maximize your potential daily. Think about it. Would you rather be *over*-qualified or *under*-qualified for a job? Would you rather be *over*-prepared or *under*-prepared for your clients? Would you prefer to be an *over*-achiever or an *under*-achiever?

It doesn't matter if you are an employee, an employer, or unemployed–you are ALWAYS the Founder, President and CEO of your own dreams. All of us have dreams that we would like to achieve. However, it's the people who take action toward their dreams that get the opportunity to fulfill and enjoy their own dreams. I have seen some extraordinary people turn their lives around just because someone told them that they were overqualified. For instance, there are entrepreneurs that started their own companies because someone told them that they were overqualified for the position that they were applying for. The next time someone tells you that you're overqualified, they might not be trying to talk you *out* of what you want to achieve. They may be secretly talking you *into* launching your own company.

Winners succeed because they learn how to maximize their personal qualities. As a winner, start looking for ways to capitalize on your personal and professional qualities. Winning is about discovering the potential that you already have *inside* of you and maximizing it. If you never use your own potential, how do you expect to win? To win in your endeavors, you will need to implement and maximize your personal and professional qualities daily.

5

BLAME YOUR SUCCESS

How many times will you blame others for your achievements?

We have all heard and seen it before. What is it? It's called the *blame game*. "It's not my fault," he or she says. Nobody likes to be wrong. Nor does every person wants to take full responsibility for his or her own actions and consequences, especially if the results are unpleasant, so he or she blames it on someone else. "Yeah, that's what we'll do," said the little girl to her little brother. "We'll blame it on dad, once mom asks who broke the vase."

If you *blame others* for your unwanted results, when are you going to start "blaming yourself?" Blaming someone else is one of the easiest things you can do because all you have to do is say, "He or she did it." Then the attention is instantly off you, so you think. However, the part that most people don't realize is that people can tell a phony when they see one, even when it comes to blaming others. In sports, you don't think the coaches and the fans can't see who is going all out and giving their best, versus who is lackadaisical and going at half speed? In business, people know who is the best salesperson in the company, and who is the weakest link at the company.

As I stated in my book, *Think Progress*, "If you didn't have anyone around you to blame for your *own* results, whom would you seek to place the blame on for your *own* results?" We are all responsible for our own results. If you want to blame others for your unwanted results, sure go ahead, and blame them for your *failures*. But, once you "succeed," whom will you blame for your *success*?

It's interesting how we will quickly blame someone else for our *failures*. However, we will delay or won't give someone credit for our *successes*. For example, when a reporter was interviewing the team captain on the football team, he was asked to talk about the touchdown that he scored. Instead of giving credit to his teammates who helped him score the touchdown, he took it upon himself to take all of the credit for the touchdown, and for their team victory. Now, let's rewind the same scenario, and put a little twist to it. When the reporter interviewed the team captain on the football team, he was asked to talk about why they *didn't* score the touchdown. What do you think his response would be? Do you think he would take all of the credit for losing the game? Or do you think he would blame his teammates for losing the game? When people fall short of what they want to achieve, they will quickly blame others for their misfortunes. Like the saying goes, "When things are going *good*, everyone wants to take the credit. Whenever something goes *bad*, no one wants to take the credit."

Dr. Denis Waitley, author and professional speaker once stated, "Whether you are a bum on skid row or a happy individual, you can pat yourself on the back, take the credit, or blame for your place in life." If you fail at something, don't let it discourage you from giving your best effort. Winners know they are responsible for their own successes and failures. This is one reason why winners refuse to blame others for their personal failures. When winners fall short of what they want to achieve, they look for new and effective resources to improve themselves, so they will succeed the next time. When your goal is to win, don't look for ways to blame others; seek ways that will lead you to succeed.

The question is not who are *you* going to blame, but what are *you* going to do, so no one blames you? As a winner, when you give your best effort, no one will blame you. When you surround yourself with the right people, no one will blame you. When you give your best effort, you will produce your best performance. The more you give your best performance, the more you will notice that you won't need to blame others, because you will find yourself winning more in your endeavors.

6

THE PROCESS OF WINNING

Success is available to you; are you ready to
go through the process?

Success has your name on it. There is nothing between you and what you want to achieve, except you physically going through the "process" to achieve it. Every winner goes through the *process* stage of learning the fundamentals of what he or she wants to achieve. It's during the *process* stage, when winners learn how to transform their internal vision into external success. As some like to call it, "Turning your dreams into reality."

Everything has a "process" attached to it. For instance, if you were to go to the store, the *process* would consist of you putting on your shoes and clothes, grabbing your house and car keys, going out the house, getting into your car, driving to the store, going into the store, retrieving the items in the store, standing in line, paying the cashier, exiting the store, getting back into your car, driving back home, opening and closing your car door, preparing your key to place into the lock of your door, turning the key, opening up the door to your home, closing the door, putting your keys down, and opening up the product that you just purchased from the store. What a process? But, at least you bought what you went to the store to buy. God forbid if you forgot something at the store, you would have to go back through the same process again.

My life changed once I became an open-minded person. Growing up, as an only child, I always knew that I wanted to be successful. As I grew from childhood into adulthood, I met various people who taught me astute ways to succeed. Though countless people have entered into and exited out of my life, every person was different and each person taught me something new. Each person showed me how to improve my own life. I didn't start making progress in my life until I went through the process. One life-changing process that I went through was when I decided to open my mind to new ideas. Believe it or not, I used to be a closed minded and skeptical person. I overcame my skepticism, when I became an open-minded person. The day I decided to open my mind to new possibilities that was the defining moment I learned how to design my own success.

As I stated on a few occasions, "There is something about learning something new that makes you want to learn more." As a winner, you must be willing to open your mind to new ideas, products, and strategies because nothing stays the same. When you become an open-minded person, it's as if you're mentally giving your mind permission to seek new possibilities. Once you become an open-minded person, you will begin to learn new concepts that will not only broaden your horizons, but will also show you how to win. Winning is a fundamental process. This is why most winners start with the basics. If you never learn the basics, you will prevent yourself from winning. Winning is not hard once you learn the fundamentals of winning. Yes, you will need to put in the work to win, but at least you will know what you will need to do to achieve your goals.

Winners know about new possibilities because they mentally visualize them. Some athletes, like Tiger Woods, visualize their forthcoming success. They call this their *visualization* process. This is when they mentally go through the process of visualizing themselves succeeding. Most Olympians are known to use the visualization process. They go into a quiet area, so they can rest their minds and bodies. Then they begin to mentally visualize their performance step-by-step, as though they were already physically performing their routine. After mentally visualizing their performance, they physically go out and perform the routine as they mentally envisioned.

As a winner, your external success is a reflection of how you mentally see yourself succeeding. This is why it's essential that you visualize yourself successfully achieving your goals and dreams. The more you envision yourself succeeding in your mind's eye, the more you will mentally condition yourself for success.

7

CLIMB FROM FAILURE

Did you take another step on your success ladder today?

If you were to look inside the archives of all the winners who reached the level of success, you would find the majority of them failed many times before they became successful.

Many of us have tried something in our lives and didn't succeed on our first attempt. I will be the first person to admit that I have attempted numerous things in my life, and a lot of my attempts were unsuccessful. For example, when I was in the United States Marine Corps (USMC), during boot camp, we had to pass various qualification tests. There was one test that kept giving me trouble. It was the swim qualification test, also known as *combat survival swimming*. You may be thinking, "What's so hard about swimming?" If you know how to swim, it's easy for you to say. But, swimming was difficult for me because I couldn't swim. Not to mention, everyone's first jump took place from a 12-ft high diving board. Yes, I was scared as I stood at the top looking down at the pool of water. I was terrified. Nonetheless, in my mind, it was a new challenge that I needed to conquer, so I jumped in the pool. I can relate with the Marine on one of the USMC commercials, when he's standing at the top of the tall diving board looking down at the pool, as he described his USMC experience. In the commercial, he states, "I faced one of the toughest challenges of my life right here. I couldn't swim. But, I could still hear my drill instructor today. 'Don't quit. If you quit now, you will always quit in life. Go for it!' So, I jumped in. Unsure. Apprehensive. And scared out of my mind. But, I came up a Marine."

Yes, I failed my swim qualification test a few times. But I was determined to succeed, and I eventually passed the swim qualification test. Although I didn't succeed the first or second time around, I refused to give up. Instead of giving up, which is the easiest thing to do in life, I conditioned my mind and actions to achieve my goals. One major lesson I learned about thinking big: Just because you failed at something doesn't mean you will always fail. Nobody enjoys failing. Nonetheless, failure is a part of life, and we must learn to grow from it.

No one was born to be a failure in life. Failure is the bumpy road to success that most people don't want to travel on to succeed. Failure grooms countless successful men and women to grow into creative thinkers and unstoppable winners. For example, there are carpenters who didn't take the right measurements on their first day at work. Although the carpenters failed the first time, they continued to take measurements, until they learned how to successfully take the right measurements. You must do the same. If you fail at something, keep going, until you succeed.

The secret to winning is to learn how to succeed from your failures. Begin to look at your failures as a learning process. If you fail, don't view yourself as a failure. Winners know "failure" is usually the first step on every success ladder. Nevertheless, they keep climbing, until they reach success. If you fail at something the first time around, don't give up! Throw out the things that *didn't* work for you. Start focusing on the things that *did* work for you. After reviewing what worked for you, get back on your success ladder. Your success is waiting for you to reach toward it. Start taking more steps forward and upward on your success ladder. The more steps you take on your success ladder, the further you will move upward.

As a winner, stand up and aim high! Look forward, upward, and beyond your failures. Start building your own success with one triumph at a time. Take a moment to write down at least one goal that you want to achieve today. After you write down your one goal, make a plan to achieve it, focus on it, and then take physical action toward it. Strive to accomplish at least one goal every day. It will be your focus, plans, actions, and results that will produce your victories. Your success ladder proves that you can succeed. When your goal is to succeed, you must keep moving forward and upward on your success ladder.

8

CHANGE MAKES THE DIFFERENCE

Change is a part of life.
Are you ready to change your life?

Everywhere you look, something is *changing*. If you're driving on the street, you will see the traffic lights changing colors (red, green, and yellow.) If you look at the clock, you will see the second hand continuously moving past each number as the time changes. Seasons change. People change. Technologies change. Lives change. What are you doing to *change* your life?

While doing my research for this book, I asked various people the previous question, "What are you doing to *change* your life?" After asking this question, I began to notice two things: First of all, the majority was surprised by my question. Secondly, I noticed the pattern of how, after some people heard the word "change," their body appeared tense. Could it have been because they viewed "change" as a bad thought or as a negative word? Maybe.

One reason underachievers don't succeed is because they are afraid to make changes in their lives. Winners understand change is a part of life. There is nothing wrong with making changes in your life. If you were to ask successful people how they succeeded, most of them would tell you that they had to make various adjustments on their road toward success. Many successful people are still making changes on their journey. Madonna, the singer, actress, mom, and entrepreneur is a good example for the word "change." Madonna always looks for new ways to reinvent herself. When Madonna reinvents herself, the transformation enhances her appearance and performance. When it comes to reinventing, you must be willing to adapt to change. You don't have to reinvent the wheel, but you must be willing to reinvent yourself. Reinventing yourself will give you the opportunity to feel like a new and improved person. What are you doing to reinvent yourself?

Winners continuously seek and discover innovative ways to keep evolving. In her book, *When Life Changes or You Wish It Would*, Carol Adrienne wrote, "When you begin to take charge of any part of your life that you have been avoiding for a long time…it's very likely you will go through a dark, overwhelming, or scary period while you change your approach." Sometimes change is needed, so you can start producing better results. To win, you must be prepared to make a few changes on your journey. It will be the changes you *make* or the changes you *refuse to make* that will lead you to succeed or fail. If making a few changes will help you prosper, why not make the changes? Small changes can make a gigantic difference in your results.

> **"It will be the changes you make or the changes you refuse to make that will lead you to succeed or fail."**

Change is the invisible superpower for success. Charles Franklin Kettering, the inventor, engineer, and entrepreneur, once said, "The world hates change, yet it is the only thing that has brought progress." Sometimes *change* is the solution. There will be times when you will need to change your game plan. When you want your life to change, don't sit down and let life change you. Stand up and change your life. If you're fearful of making a few adjustments in your life, how do you expect to win? If you're afraid of the word "change," don't strive for *change*–strive for "improvement." Once you start *improving* yourself, you will eventually change.

As a winner, you will need to put forth the effort to change your actions and results to succeed. Take a moment and ask yourself, "What do I need to change in my life?" Keep in mind, effective results come from making a few changes. For example, if you want to lose weight, make a *change* in your eating habits. If you want to enhance your finances, make a *change* in your spending habits. If you want to improve your relationships, make a *change* in your communication skills. You will win, once you make the necessary changes in your life.

9

WHO'S HOLDING YOUR KEYS?

Did you turn the key to your success today?

If you lost everything that you owned (money, home, car, job, relationship, etc.) you would still have the "keys" to succeed in your life. The first key to winning in life is to understand that *you* hold the master keys to your own success.

Many people go through life with limits because they have given others control over their personal lives. Controlled limits will minimize your creativity, results, and success. No one controls your life except *you*. Never limit yourself by giving someone else power over your personal limits. You have too much potential to have limits placed on you.

Allow me to show you how much control you have over your life and success by using a "lock and key" scenario. First of all, the only people who have access to your life are the people that *you* issue a key to enter your life. For example, let's say that you just bought a brand new house. At the beginning, you are the only person with the key to your house. One day you receive a call from a friend. Your friend lets you know that he or she will be coming in town for a few days, so you invite him or her to stay with you while in town. Before your friend's arrival date, you go to a nearby locksmith and get an additional key made for your friend. Once your friend arrives in town, you give him or her the additional key. If you notice, your friend did <u>not</u> have access to your house, until *you* gave him or her a key to enter your house.

The same scenario happens every time you have an encounter with someone. Every person that you meet doesn't have access to enter your life. A person doesn't have complete access into your life until you give him or her complete access to enter into your life. In other words, *you* are the gatekeeper, which means you have the first and final say to the people that you allow into your personal space. It's that simple. Your friends are fortunate, because you have personally issued them a special key to enter into your life.

As a winner, you hold the master keys to your own life and success. Don't give your keys to just anyone or anything. Think about it. You wouldn't give your house or car keys to a stranger, so why would you give your "life" keys to random people? Give your keys to trustworthy people who will add value to your life. One of the keys to success is doing what it takes to succeed. When you want to know where *you* stand in life take a look at the people, places and things around you. Are the *people* around you using positive or negative language? Are the *places* you're visiting inspiring you or depressing you? Are the *things* in your life helping you advance or sidetracking you? Who are the people helping you succeed? Who are the people hurting your success? How many people are optimistic? Who is pessimistic?

As a winner, start asking yourself, "Is it time for me to clean house?" If so, begin the process. One way to enjoy a clean house is by removing the clutter. When you clean out your closet, you usually throw away the things you no longer need. As you begin to clean up your life, start eliminating the negative people, places, and things out of your life. Once you throw out the negativity, you will make room for the right people to enter your life. It's always good to have the right people around you, because they will help you win. Remember, when you *seek the best* people, places, and things–you will *discover the best* people, places, and things.

Yes, I am aware that this chapter is called *"Who's Holding Your Keys?"* However, I would like to paraphrase it with *"Who's Holding Your Piece Of The Puzzle?"* Whatever you are looking for it's looking for you too. Life is like an endless jigsaw puzzle. As a winner, you must continuously seek and find the missing pieces, and place them correctly into your life. Some pieces (people and places) won't fit into certain areas of your life puzzle. That's okay. Keep seeking until you discover the right pieces that will fit into your life.

10

VOLUME OF DETERMINATION

Do you have your determination volume on high, low, mute, or off?

One day, while having lunch with an intelligent and successful friend name Diane, I asked her a simple question, "Out of all the adversity that you've been through in your life, what steps did you take to overcome your challenges?" The answer she gave me was a breathtaking and an empowering response. She replied, "I always knew what I wanted to achieve, so I always fed my vision with pure determination and action until I achieved it." In conclusion, Diane stated, "I never limited my vision with boundaries because I stretched my boundaries with my determination to succeed."

Boundaries don't exist in the mind of winners. Winners prevail by using their determination to overcome their obstacles. All of us encounter some form of adversity. Many people let their adversity defeat them by giving up. Giving up is never an option or a solution for winners. Yes, there will be times when you will face defeat. But, never let defeat beat you because you gave up. Winners refuse to give up. That's why they are winners. Winners could have their backs pushed against the walls, but they will not give up. Underachievers give up. Winners prevail. You are not an underachiever. You are a *winner*, which means giving up is not an option.

> *"Yes, there will be times when you will face defeat.*
> *But, never let defeat beat you because you gave up."*

When you encounter challenges in your life that is one of the best times to turn up the volume on your determination, so you can prevail. Determination is a personal commitment that you make inside of yourself to succeed. When you're determined to succeed, nothing or no one will be able to stop you from accomplishing your mission. When the game is on the line and your objective is to win the big game, you must be willing to mentally, emotionally, and physically dig deeper within yourself to turn your determination volume all the way up to the highest level. This is also known as "The Peak Performance Level." It's the "peak" performance versus the "weak" performance that separates the winners from the losers.

Determination is in the DNA of winners. Winners are driven to succeed because they are determined to succeed. Winners know success is attained via determination, action, results and persistence–not through procrastination and excuses. Your *excuses and procrastination* will keep you from succeeding. Your *determination and persistence* will keep you moving onward until you succeed. Your determination is the fuel that ignites your inner drive. When you merge your determination, action and persistence together you will become an unstoppable winner.

When you want to achieve something, don't wait for it to happen. When your goal is to win, you must stand up, step on the field with pure "determination" and make it happen.

- It will be your *determination* that will continuously place you across the achievement line.
- It will be your *determination* that will push you when your body is aching with pain.
- It will be your *determination* that will empower you to go beyond your personal challenges.
- It will be your *determination* that will make you discover yourself.
- It will be your *determination* that will make you give your best performance.
- It will be your *determination* that will place the smile on your face when you say, "I won."

As a winner, you have too much determination within you to give up. *Turn on and turn up* the volume on your actions, determination and persistence. The louder you turn up the volume on your determination, the more you will hear the sound of victory.

11

LIVE YOUR DREAMS, NOT YOUR NIGHTMARES

How much attention are you giving to your own dreams?

Richard DeVos, the co-founder of *Amway* and the owner of the NBA Orlando Magic basketball team, once stated, "If you have a dream, give it a chance to happen." Are you living your dreams? Or are you afraid to dream? Most winners are called "dreamers."

It's the winners who fulfill their dreams. Many of us have big dreams. While some of us have small dreams. But overall, all of us have dreams that we want to personally achieve. Dream big, dream differently, but never stop dreaming.

One effective way to win is to "dream big." Every successful person was once upon a time called a *dreamer*. It's the dreamers who make the world go around. There are billions of people throughout the world. However, while everyone else is sleeping in bed counting sheep, it's the dreamers who are waking up and taking action toward their dreams. Winners do more than dream big, they take action toward their big dreams daily. How many times have you heard winners say, "It was exactly how I *dreamed* it would be?" It's the dreamers like Sam Walton and Mary Kay Ash, who turned their *Sam's Club, Walmart, and Mary Kay* dreams into reality, which continues to make a difference globally. It's a dreamer like Howard Schultz, who turned *Starbucks Coffee* into a household brand worldwide. It's dreamers like Russell Simmons and Earvin "Magic" Johnson who continue to make a difference in the urban communities. Walt Disney, who created an entire dreamland called *Disneyland,* once stated, "If you can dream it, you can do it." It's the dreamers who are constantly thinking and saying, "There has to be a better way!"

Visions are limitless! There is a Japanese proverb that says, "Vision without action is a daydream. Action without vision is a nightmare." The majority of successful people who reached astonishing heights started with a big vision. There are first-generation wealthy people who started out financially broke with only a dream. Nonetheless, they turned their dreams into millions and billions of dollars. Winners use their creative minds to explore and develop new ways to transform their mental visions into forthcoming success.

Winners are action-oriented. Your dreams are achievable when you apply action toward them. It's never too early or too late to transform your dreams into reality. When you have a dream, don't sit on it. Stand up and go for your dreams. You never know, your dreams could set the next trend that will make a difference in the world. As a winner, always remember, your dreams are too valuable to waste. When you refuse to take physical action toward your dreams, they will remain just a vision in your mind. Don't let your dreams stay asleep inside of you. Awake your dreams with action. Start taking physical steps toward your dreams. It will be your physical actions toward your mental vision that will make your dreams come true.

Some people will tell you, "Your dreams are *impossible*." As a winner, you must believe your dreams are *possible*. Most of the people who utter, "Your dreams are impossible" are the same people who never fulfilled their own dreams. Are you going to stop striving toward *your* dreams just because someone didn't fulfill his or her own dreams? It's been said, "Live without regrets." The biggest regret for most people is not fulfilling or enjoying their own dreams. They have lived everyone else's dream, but they forgot to live their own dreams. Whatever you do, don't let that be you. As a winner, always strive to live and enjoy your own dreams.

Like a baby needs attention, your *dreams* need attention too. Your dreams are designed for you to physically live them. Dream big! Don't shortchange your dreams. Take the necessary actions that will make your dreams become a reality. *Thinking* about your dreams will keep them in your head. *Applying physical action* toward your dreams will make your dreams come to existence. Starting today, physically step into your own dreams…Live Your Dreams!

12

BALANCE YOUR SELF-APPOINTMENTS

Did you make an appointment with yourself today?

Did you look at your schedule today? If so, what did you see? Did you see that you have a meeting at 9:00 am? Did you see that you're scheduled to have lunch with your best friend at 12:00 pm? Did you see that you have a conference call at 2:45 pm? Did you see that you have a doctor's appointment at 4:00 pm? Did you see it's your turn to pick-up the kids from practice at 5:30 pm? It's amazing how much we try to juggle within 24 hours. While you put in countless hours tackling chores and completing tasks, you also need to make a *self-appointment.*

A self-appointment is an allotted time for you to relax and rejuvenate your mind and body from all the hustle and bustle. Do you know someone who persistently works long hours at a job doing for others, yet he or she forgets to make time for oneself? It's interesting how we can make time to work for others and find time to balance our checkbooks, but we forget to make time to balance our own lives. There is nothing wrong with doing things for others. However, there is something wrong when we refuse to do things for ourselves.

Balance is an area of life countless people overlook daily. Rather than doing things that would add balance, some of us continue to look for ways to make our lives unbalanced by taking on more chores. Balance is a necessity. Your life may currently look like an unbalanced seesaw, but you can add balance into your life. When you add balance to your life you will minimize fatigue and stress. Balance is not only meant for time management. Balance is also used for discovering new ways to add excitement into your life, instead of constantly running all over the place.

You may be thinking, "How can I add balance to my life?" One effective way is by making a "self-appointment." You make appointments with others (doctor, dentist, hair stylist, etc.), but when was the last time you made an appointment with *yourself*? You are an important person, so start treating yourself as such. As an important person, you need quality time. Make time in your schedule for a *self-appointment*, so you can reward yourself with quality time. Sometimes the best solution is to simply take a break, so your mind can take a break too. Many of us need to let ourselves know that it's okay to mentally and physically remove ourselves away from people, places, and things for a few minutes, hours, or days. The fresh breathing space will give you the opportunity to relax, gather your thoughts together and have some "me" time.

> *"Sometimes the best solution is to simply take a break, so your mind can take a break too."*

Making a *self-appointment* is one of the best gifts that you could ever give to yourself. Reward yourself with a self-appointment today. Select a time and location where you can relax for at least 10 to 30 minutes without interruptions. If you need more time, you can extend the duration of your self-appointment. The time you spend alone–without interruptions–will allow you to build inner peace. In addition, it will provide you with the opportunity to spend quality time with yourself, so you can relax your mind and body, add pleasure in your life, discover better solutions, and rejuvenate your internal strength to grow as a person.

Winners like to use the self-appointment technique because it gives them the opportunity to become more productive. Some winners use their self-appointments for meditation (time for reflection) or simply relaxation. As a winner, look at your schedule and find a time that you can make a daily self-appointment. Once you make a *self-appointment*, keep the appointment with yourself. Each self-appointment will do more than give you the opportunity to relax your mind, body and soul. It will strengthen your inner stability and enable you to discover something new about yourself, as well as it will enhance your life and productivity.

13

YOU NEVER KNOW

Even when you think you know, do you really know?

A few years ago, I had an office inside of the Empire State building in New York City. One day, during working hours, I was on the elevator to my office. While on the elevator, there was a well-dressed gentleman in business attire. His suit, shirt and tie were all neatly pressed. His shoes were highly polished, as he held onto the handle of his fashionable briefcase.

On the warm summer day, I was wearing casual clothing–khaki trousers, a buttoned-down collared shirt, and loafer shoes. Since it was only the businessman and I on the elevator, I attempted to make small talk with the gentleman by mentioning the weather. My small talk wasn't too successful. The well-dressed man refused to respond to the comments that I made about the weather. I've always heard, "You can never go wrong when you talk about the weather with someone." I guess I should find the person who created that statement, so I can inquire, "What environment were they talking about when they stated that you can never go wrong when you talk about the weather with someone?"

The elevator stopped on the 33rd floor. As the elevator doors opened, the gentleman (Mr. Business attire) and I both exited on the same floor. Still silent, without saying a single word to me, Mr. Business attire exited the elevator first with his ego leading the way. He entered the office with an instant smile on his face, requesting to see the decision-maker of a particular company. As the receptionist was responding to Mr. Business attire, she noticed me walking in the front door of the office. The receptionist smiled and acknowledged me by saying, "Hello Mr. Williams, I thought you were on vacation." I responded to the receptionist, "I forgot something in my office."

The receptionist stated to Mr. Business attire, "Sir, Mr. Williams is the decision-maker of the company that you're inquiring about.

He is the owner of the company." Can you imagine the look on Mr. Business attire's face once he found out that I was the person that he needed to see and speak with at the company? I was on the elevator with him the entire time. Nonetheless, Mr. Business attire refused to talk to me on the elevator because he judged the clothing I was wearing at the moment.

The moral of the story: You never know the importance of the people around you, so make it your duty to be polite to every person that you meet. As the Golden Rule states, "Do unto others as you would have them do unto you." In other words, treat others how you want to be treated. If you want respect, treat others with respect. Mary Kay Ash, the founder of Mary Kay Cosmetics once stated, "When I meet someone, I imagine her wearing an invisible sign that says, 'Make me feel important.'" The more you make others feel important, the more you will reward yourself by feeling important too. As I'm writing, one of Zig Ziglar's famous quotes come to mind: "You can get everything in life you want if you help enough people get what they want."

Everyone wants to feel needed and important, so give them what they want...make them feel special and important. For example, I can recall the first time I met the NBA Hall of Famer, Earvin "Magic" Johnson in New York. As I was walking out of the hotel, he was walking into the hotel, so I held the door for him as he entered. As he thanked me—with his signature smile—he asked me, "How's your family?" Although, Magic didn't know me personally, he still made me feel important with a simple inquiry. What could you do today to make someone feel important?

As a winner, always think with your own "mind," and not with your "ego." When you think with your *ego*, you may overlook what you're looking for. When you think with your own *mind*, you will discover what you're looking for. Remember the Golden Rule. Place yourself in the shoes of others. Then seek ways to make the person feel important, valuable, and special.

14

THE ENTRANCE TO SUCCESS MOUNTAIN

If you had your own success door, would you open or close it?

Every success has an entrance to it. Imagine yourself standing in a very long line at an amusement park waiting to ride the world's most highly anticipated roller coaster. The roller coaster is called *Success Mountain.*

Many people are standing in front of you waiting to ride the renowned roller coaster, and it seems as though the line hasn't moved in about two hours. As you stand in the humid weather, you find yourself getting thirsty and tired. While standing in the hot sun and lengthy line, you have three choices. The three choices are as follows:

1. You could step out of the long line, go buy something to eat and drink, and sit down in the shade.
2. You could continue to stand in the long line, and eventually get on the "GREATEST" ride ever made.
3. You could leave the amusement park, go home, and never think about the ride again in your life.

Out of the three choices, which <u>one</u> would you choose? This is an ordeal countless people encounter on a daily basis. No one ever said, "Success will be an easy task." However, every second of every day there are millions of people throughout the world standing in an invisible lengthy line waiting for the world's best ride.

If you want to get on this highly endorsed ride, you first must walk through an opening to get on the ride. The opening is called, "The Entrance to Success Mountain." Yes, *The Entrance to Success Mountain!* The reason countless people are willing to stand at the entrance to Success Mountain is because they know it's the starting point that other successful people before them entered to reach success. Also, they know Success Mountain is the best ride ever made in the world, which will lead them to numerous exciting and adventurous destinations like happiness, wealth, success, and a better life.

"The winners in life are mountain climbers."

As the famous motivational speaker and author, Zig Ziglar, always says, "See you at the top." In order for you to reach the elite level, you will need to work your way to the top. The more you keep improving your skills and upgrading yourself to the next level, the closer you will get to reaching the pinnacle of success. If you knew your "success" was at the summit of a mountain, what would you do? Would you put on a pair of hiking boots and start climbing toward the top? Or would you stay at the bottom and say, "The mountain is too high to climb?" The winners in life are mountain climbers. Winners are always willing to climb mountains and overcome their challenges, regardless of the altitude.

Winners always strive to win–that is why they are called *winners*. How many winners do you know that enjoy losing? Probably zero, because winners refuse to lose. Winners do whatever it takes to win. One secret to winning is doing the things that will lead you to succeed. As a winner, put on your hiking boots, and keep looking for new and better paths to hoist yourself to the next level. One level you will enjoy is personal fulfillment. When you accomplish your personal goals, you will give yourself personal gratification. The more you fulfill your personal goals, the more your personal accomplishments and rewards will be endless. The ride is worth the wait. Stay in line. Before you know it, it will be your turn to enter and ride *Success Mountain*.

15

A SMILING HEART

What one thing would you do for free?

How often do you see people *smiling*? Why do you think they are smiling? Could they be smiling because they hit the lottery jackpot? Could they be smiling because they are doing what they love? There are numerous reasons to smile. One reason most people smile is because they are engaged in an activity that makes them feel good inside.

Confucius, the Greek philosopher, once said, "Wherever you go, go with all your heart." One effective way to succeed is to do the things that will continuously give you personal satisfaction. In other words, do what you love and love what you do. Winners always do what they love. Many people ask, "When do you know that you're doing what you love to do?" You will know you're doing what you love, because your heart will smile when you do it. You will know when you're doing what you love when you stop paying attention to the time. It's one thing to have time management, but when you love what you're doing, and doing what you love to do, it's not about managing your time–it's about finding more time to do the things you love. When you adore what you do, you're constantly thinking and dreaming about it. For instance, if someone tried to distract you from what you enjoy doing, you would quickly excuse yourself by politely saying, "I need to get back to work" or "I need to get back to what I was doing."

It's been said that when you love what you do, it's as if you're not working at all. I concur. When you do what you love and love what you do, it's not work–it's enjoyment. Winners love what they do so much that they are willing to make sacrifices in their lives, so they can do more of what they love to do. Winners deliberately make more time to do the things they love doing, even if they aren't paid to do it. Most winners love what they do so much that they would literally do it for free. When winners do what they love, they feel like they are on vacation every day.

I love what I do so much that I can't wait to do it again the next day. This explains why I stay up late at night and wake up early in the morning, because I am constantly doing what I love. When people ask me why I have a smile on my face, I simply reply, "Because I'm doing what I love to do every day." Can you say the same thing? When you wake up in the morning, are you doing exactly what you *love* to do? If not, why not? What's holding you back? What needs to happen for you to start doing what you love? Only you can answer these questions, because it starts with *you*. You are the only person who knows what makes you happy. Now that you know you're the originator of your own happiness, start doing the things that you love to do.

Winners don't wait for the perfect moment–they enjoy every moment. Stop waiting for the "perfect" moment. Take action now! Now is the perfect opportunity for you to go out and experience what you have always wanted to achieve in your life. *Waiting* will keep you from moving forward. *Waiting* will make you waste valuable time. *Waiting* will hinder you from enjoying the good life. Why would you want to prolong doing what you love when the opportunity is present now? There are so many opportunities around us that we tend to overlook the opportunities around us.

There are countless people who go through life dreaming about doing the things that they would love to do, but they never take action toward their dreams. Don't let that be you. Don't become an "I *can't* succeed" victim, because you *can* succeed. If others have succeeded, so *can* you!

As a winner, you need to discover what you love to do, and start doing it. This is one way to make your heart smile. When you do what you love and love what you do, you will always stand out as a winner. Why? Because when you do what you love, you will continue to do whatever it takes to do more of it. Remember, as a winner, you are always in charge of the height and width of your own personal happiness and success. What will you do to make your heart smile?

16

BUILD YOUR ALL-STAR TEAM

*Who do you have on your team that will help you
win the big game?*

One day an executive asked his Human Resources Director if everything was okay? The HR Director replied, "Yes, why did you ask?" The executive stated, "I've noticed the quality of our hiring has decreased." Baffled by what she had just heard, the HR Director inquired, "What do you mean?" The executive replied, "If we aren't hiring the best people to add to our team, not only will we lose, but all of us will soon be out of a job."

Every game plan, including the best game plan, needs the right players on the team to win the big game. Life is the game. What are you doing to win in life? What are you doing to create better results for yourself? One way you can produce better results is by creating and building your own success team. Surrounding yourself with winners will give you the opportunity to become one of the elite. Winners know that the elite people have the resources and skills that will help them produce first-class results. Affiliating yourself with intelligent, optimistic, and enthusiastic people will give you an advantage, because you will learn firsthand how to succeed.

One effective way to enter the winner's circle is to place yourself in the winner's circle. Surrounding yourself with other winners will do more than give you the opportunity to rub elbows with them. It will enable you to receive first-class wisdom, as you bounce your ideas off them. When you ask winners questions such as, "How did you succeed?" "What steps did you take to succeed?" "What advice would you give to someone who would like to reach your level of success?" you will begin to place yourself in the circle of winners. Winners like helping others win too. Once you begin to ask winners questions, they will commence to share their unique strategies with you, which will advance your creative intelligence, actions, and results to win. The more winners that you surround yourself with, the more you will learn how to win.

The key to winning is to keep upgrading and encircling yourself with the best people. As a winner, start associating yourself with a diverse group of winners, because each person and group will teach you new and effective ways to achieve your personal and professional goals.

When you surround yourself with the best, it will give you the opportunity to learn, borrow, and absorb their unique wisdom, strategies, and principles to enhance your own success. Build a relationship with the people who can and will help you succeed. Associate yourself with mastermind individuals who have the resources and skills to multiply your potential and skills.

The acronym for TEAM is Together Everyone Achieves More. All dreams have a *team*. A tennis player, a boxer, and a gymnast are all individuals. However, they all have a *team* to help them win. Who do you have on your *team*? Are they helping you win or lose? Are they optimistic or pessimistic? Are they helping you reach the next level or are they trying to pull you down a few levels? Select the people who will help you reach the *next* level. Create your own all-star success team. An all-star success team consists of a diverse group of people who are creative, supportive, and positive thinkers. Your all-star success team will help transform your dreams and goals into success. Each member on your team will present his or her own uniqueness, which will add versatility, balance, and value to the group. It will be the people on your all-star success team that will help you succeed, so make sure you select the right and the best people for your team.

As a winner, your all-star success team will need to believe in you. Likewise, they will need to provide you with the most effective resources. Look for positive, realistic thinkers, and people who will share their creative minds and techniques with you. Start with one person. Then add more resourceful people onto your all-star success team. Remember the acronym for TEAM: Together Everyone Achieves More. The more winners (elite thinkers) that you add to your success team, the more you will discover, build, and multiply new ways to win in your endeavors.

17

FREE YOUR MIND

Will you lock or unlock your creative mind today?

Marcus Aurelius, the author of *Meditations*, was correct when he wrote, "Our life is what our thoughts make it." Whenever we let "limiting" words, thoughts, people, places, and distractions enter our minds, we voluntarily allow each of them to place a limited ceiling on top of our mental visions, creativity, and physical potential.

Winners are free-minded people who allow their minds to roam without restraints. When the mind is kept from exploring new concepts, it becomes trapped inside of a mental limitation. A *mental limitation* is like an invisible cage. Though there are no physical bars, fences, locks, or chains in the vicinity, many people mentally *limit* themselves by placing their state of mind inside an invisible cage, which limits them from succeeding.

How many people do you know with low self-esteem? Most people with low self-esteem neglect to open their invisible cage, because they have mentally trapped themselves within their own minds. Prisoners may have their freedom restricted from the *outside* world. However, a lot of people on the *outside* world have placed themselves "inside" a mental prison by restricting their own mental freedom. There are people who literally think others are holding them back from their personal freedom. For example, a gentleman once told me that his boss, friends, and loved ones all limited him. The people around him didn't place limits on him, he mentally placed limitations on himself. Winners refuse to place limits on themselves. The only limit to winners is the "speed limit." Every limit starts with oneself. It's interesting how we look everywhere else, even outside of ourselves for limiting factors, but we refuse to see the mass of limitations that we are constantly placing on ourselves. In order to win, we must stop mentally self-sabotaging ourselves.

"A limited mind will always look for minimum and limited results, because that is all it knows what to seek."

Winners don't prevail because they *limit* their thoughts. Winners prevail because they *alter* their thoughts. A limited mind will always look for minimum and limited results, because that is all it knows what to seek. Having a limited mind will place limits on everything around you. When you limit your beliefs, you start to doubt yourself. When you doubt yourself, you limit the levels of your own success. Your personal success starts with the limits of your personal beliefs. *You* are the only person with the master key to your own invisible cage. You have a choice: You can either have a *limited* mind or you can *free* your mind. When you remove the doubts and limits from your mind, and begin to open your mind and believe in yourself, you will free your mind to succeed in your endeavors.

Your mind is like a custom-made suit. You can select the fabric, color, length, and design to how you want it to look. The same applies with your mind. You can select the words, thoughts, visions, and mindset to how you want your life and success to look. Will you place limits on your mind? Or will you remove the limits from your mind?

As a winner, you must remove the limits from your mind. The key to freeing your mind is to open your mind to new possibilities. When you think you have a long way to go to achieve your goals, dreams, and ideas, you might be just one step away from achieving them. There is an advantage to freeing your mind. When you free your own mind, you can achieve whatever you want to achieve in your life. Open your mind to new possibilities. Think bigger. Imagine yourself being victorious. Push beyond your limits. Once you remove your limits, you will instantly become limitless. When you remove your *mental* ceiling, you will see the sky is the limit.

18

POWER OF CONFIDENCE

It takes confidence to win! How full is your bucket of confidence?

Every winner is equipped with something exceptional that makes him or her stand out from everyone else. Oprah Winfrey and Donald Trump are very successful people. Besides their wealth and hard work, there is one distinction that continues to make them stand out from the crowd. It's their *self-confidence.*

The high achievers who reach extraordinary levels in their professional and personal lives are the people who walk, talk, breathe, perform and present themselves with confidence. All winners strongly believe in themselves. Winners know that if they don't believe in themselves they could lose. One secret about winners: Winners refuse to lose. Winners do whatever it takes to win. Winners know there are various ways to win, but having self-confidence is mandatory to win.

Winners use their self-confidence as one of their core strengths. Self-confidence is the empowering factor that ignites winners' internal fuel to excel toward excellence. Without self-confidence, we defeat ourselves. With self-confidence, we conquer our defeats. Winners are like warriors–they conquer their defeats. As a winner, it's essential that you have self-confidence. Self-confidence entails believing in oneself. The more you believe in yourself, the more you will enhance your self-confidence. The more you believe in yourself, the more you will conquer your fears. The more you believe in yourself, the more you will succeed. The level of your self-confidence will play a vital factor in the height of your success.

> *"Without self-confidence, we defeat ourselves.*
> *With self-confidence, we conquer our defeats."*

As a winner, you will double your opportunities to win once you build up your self-confidence. To win, you will need to raise your self-confidence from low to high. Low self-confidence is equivalent to having low self-esteem. Did you know that *low self-esteem* is a disease? In his compelling book, *Think Like a Winner*, Dr. Walter Doyle Staples wrote, "The most wide spread and debilitating disease in the world today is not cancer, it's not heart disease, and it's not AIDS. It's low self-esteem brought on by a poor self-image." If you have low self-esteem, you can upgrade it to high self-esteem by enhancing your self-image. Your self-image is an internal reflection of how you mentally envision yourself. If you have low self-esteem, start visualizing yourself with high self-esteem. Once you alter the way you mentally see yourself, you will begin to raise your self-esteem. When was the last time you upgraded your self-esteem? When you improve the quality of your self-esteem–from *low* self-esteem to *high* self-esteem–you will elevate yourself to new heights.

When you want to make a difference in the world, you first must start making a difference *within* yourself. You can start with your self-esteem. Building your self-esteem will develop your self-confidence. Building your self-confidence will not only build a stronger you, it will also help you build a stronger and better society.

As a winner, your self-confidence is your leverage in life. Your self-confidence is contagious. When people see that you have confidence in yourself, your confidence will rub off on them, which will boost their self-confidence. Live your life with confidence! Don't be afraid to display your own self-confidence. Your self-confidence will attract the right people into your life. Your self-confidence will give you the leverage to prevail. With your new and improved self-confidence, start telling yourself, "I am a winner!" and mean every word of it. When you say what you mean, and mean what you say, you will exude the power of your self-confidence.

19

IDENTICAL TWINS

You look familiar. Do we know each other?

Yes, we look different from each other on the "outside." We have different colored skin, body shapes, facial features, and vary in height and weight. We are different genders (male and female). We live different lifestyles. We have different ideas, dreams, and opinions. We have different attitudes. We even speak different languages. But, overall, on the "inside," we are all *identical twins*.

One evening while riding the New York City subway, I noticed a sign that said, "We are all connected." At first, I was a little skeptical of the statement, but as I continued to look at the sign I thought to myself, "What if the sign had some truth to it?" As the thought, "We are all connected," continued to linger in my mind, I looked around at my fellow subway riders. I observed how various people on the subway were quiet, while others read books, magazines and newspapers, listened to music via headphones, and talked to other passengers. Then I started to notice that we are all connected in a way. For example, the majority of us want happiness, love, success, trustworthy friends, financial independence, and gratifying relationships. We all want to have and add more fun into our lives. We want to have at least one nice and reliable vehicle. We all want a comfortable home to live in. We all want the best for our families. We want to travel to different states and countries. Overall, we all want to have the best things life has to offer us.

Everyone is looking for someone or something to connect with. It's interesting how one person can think and say, "I'm better than you" when all of us have the potential to be successful. I'm amazed at how some people will talk negative about someone else, but they don't want others to talk negative about them. Yes, we may look different from each other. Yes, we may speak in different languages. Yes, many of us have jobs, while some people are jobless and/or homeless. But, once you go beyond all the so-called *differences*, how different are we really from each other? No matter how hard we try, none of us are perfect. As human beings, all of us have one or a few flaws in our lives. Here is an area many people don't like to think or talk about: All of us need a little help (assistance) somewhere in our lives to succeed.

> *"The more you strive to improve yourself as an individual, the more you will grow as a person."*

If we are constantly trying to distance ourselves from others, how will we grow as a society? A valuable lesson you need to understand about the word "growth" is that growth comes from *improvement.* One effective way to become a winner is to continuously improve yourself. How can you improve yourself? Get connected! The more you strive to improve yourself as an individual, the more you will grow as a person. The more we strive to improve ourselves as people, the more we will grow as a society.

As a winner, start connecting yourself with other winners. It's been said, "We become who we surround ourselves with." Who are you surrounding yourself with? Are you encircling yourself with winners or underachievers? Winners are constantly setting high standards for themselves and the people around them. When you set higher standards for yourself, others will follow your lead and upgrade their standards. If the people that you are surrounding yourself with aren't raising their standards, it may be time for you to upgrade your circle of friends. It's one thing to have friends around you that will keep you balanced and humble. It's another thing, when you have people around you that keep you unbalanced and stressed out. You will begin to achieve more, once you start connecting yourself with the right people who will help you win in your endeavors.

20

THE PLEASURE OF FUN

How often do you add fun into your life?

In his straightforward book, *It's Called WORK For A Reason*, Larry Winget wrote, "It is a solid business principle that people who enjoy what they do are better at what they do. People who do not enjoy what they do are just never going to be as good at their jobs as people who love their jobs." The winners who love their jobs and lives are usually the people who have the most fun in those areas. They even say, "I love my job" and "I love my life." If you're not having fun at your job or enjoying your life, it may be time for you to seek and discover something that you do love, so you can start having fun and enjoying it.

As kids, we visualized ourselves being successful. We even knew what we wanted to succeed in. Can you recall how you used to visualize yourself succeeding while at the playground, on the swings, and riding the seesaw? You would announce your dreams to everyone who would listen. Do you remember how you couldn't wait until someone asked, "What do you want to be when you grow up?" With a gigantic smile on your face, you quickly told them about your happy and fun-filled vision of success. As you reminisce, do you remember something that you always wanted to do since you were a little kid? What were your childhood mental visions? Do you revisit those visions as an adult? If so, do those visions still make you smile?

When it comes to working at a job, do you work for the *money*? Or do you work for the *pleasure* that the job will give you? The majority of the people that go to work don't really like their jobs, but they continue to go to the same jobs they dislike just to say the words, "I have a job." There is nothing wrong with having a job, especially if you enjoy it and have fun at your job. However, there is something wrong when you're just going through the motions and wasting everyone's time, including your own time and energy.

Have you ever noticed how some people will quickly talk about how much "money" they make working at their jobs? But, you will hardly ever hear the same people talk about how much "pleasure" their jobs give them. Although they are making money, their job is not paying them *pleasure*. There are plenty of successful people who have a lot of money. Nonetheless, wealth doesn't satisfy all of them, nor does it reward them with self-fulfillment. Some people stress out over losing a penny. While some people gain *pleasure* when they give thousands of dollars away. A few years ago, I came across an interesting article in the newspaper. The article mentioned how an anonymous man walked into a homeless shelter and gave away $35,000 to people he didn't know. He simply stated, "Use the money productively toward building a better life for yourself and family."

Winners don't succeed because they are the most talented, smartest, or the wealthiest. Most winners succeed because they are doing what they love to do. In other words, they have discovered their fun factor. What is your fun factor? What do you enjoying doing? Fun and self-fulfillment comes from doing the things that you enjoy. If you aren't enjoying what you're doing, why are you doing it? It may be time for you to seek and discover your fun factor. There are an abundance of jobs, activities, and opportunities throughout the world that are waiting for you to enjoy them. Sometimes the *fun* is in the challenge. Start challenging yourself to become more adventurous. Be more spontaneous. Do something different today. Go swing on the swings.

Today, we may be a little older, but we are still kids at heart. As Donald Trump once stated, "I don't work. I have fun." As a winner, you can work and have fun at the same time. It's okay to have fun. Let your inner child out by adding fun into your life. Imagine yourself having more fun. Write down a few goals that you think will add fun into your life. Read them daily. After reading your goals, start taking action toward your vision of fun on a daily basis.

21

TRADITIONALLY SPEAKING

If you could change a tradition,
which tradition would you change?

There are so many traditions around the world that it will make you stop and say, "WOW! Is that a tradition too?" Just because something is called a "tradition" doesn't make it right. There have been numerous times when I've personally disagreed with someone about something, then the person replied, "It's a *tradition*." Although most traditions started years ago, many of them still exist today, while some of the traditions have now become taboo.

The majority of all traditions have been handed down from generations. For example, many years ago, it used to be a *tradition* for people to sit around the radio, and listen to their favorite entertainers. Times have changed, technology has changed, and so have we. Today, in the 21st century, we can literally see and hear our favorite entertainers, actors and actresses in the comfort of our homes while enjoying them via our personal TV, cable and/or satellite, DVD, and Internet without ever walking out of the house.

Once upon a time, there was a *tradition,* when women could only be secretaries in the corporate world. Today, you have men who are secretaries, and women owning their own companies. There was a *tradition,* when people thought they had to attend college first just to receive a degree before starting their own companies. Today, there are successful entrepreneurs who have never attended college, nor received a college degree, but have employees with college degrees working for them.

"We are living in a new era, which means every tradition
can be changed or improved."

Speaking of traditions, how many times have you heard someone say, "My culture is such and such, so I am supposed to act this way?" Some traditions are so outdated that they need to be revised. There is nothing wrong with having traditions. However, there is something wrong with a tradition when you disagree with the tradition. We are living in a new era, which means every tradition can be changed or improved. Think about it. Someone had to first call something a "tradition" to make it a *tradition*. If you really wanted to, you could modify the tradition. If you don't want to change the tradition, why not add to the tradition, so you can understand and enjoy the tradition?

When it comes to traditions, winners are known to create their own traditions. A tradition to a winner is his or her own habits and rituals. If you observe winners, you will notice they do the same things over and over again. Why? Because they have created their own personal traditions. For example, whenever professional basketball players shoot a free throw, they dribble the basketball the same amount of times before they shoot the basketball into the basket.

In his book, *The Magic of Thinking Big*, Dr. David J. Schwartz asserted, "Nothing grows in ice. If we let tradition freeze our minds, new ideas can't sprout." You can transform old traditions into new traditions. As a winner, what are you doing to establish your *own* traditions? What new habits and new traditions are you personally creating for yourself to win in life? You can make your own traditions and habits simply by creating new standards and new expectations for yourself to strive toward. Don't be standard. *Raise* your standards. Get in the habit of setting standards that will challenge you daily. Get in the habit of finishing what you start. Get in the habit of creating better habits. Get in the habit of surrounding yourself with other winners. Get in the habit of expecting good things to happen in your life. When you develop your own traditions, you will start creating your own victories.

22

CHEERS! I'LL THINK TO THAT

How many times did you cheer for yourself today?

Bishop Fulton J. Sheen, one stated, "Live each day as you would climb a mountain. An occasional glance toward the summit keeps the goal in mind, but many beautiful scenes are to be observed from each new vantage point." Winners know there is always a next level. Regardless of what level you are currently on or where you are located in your life, you can aim higher, and you can live a better life.

Every person gets challenged in life, including winners. Many people can handle their challenges, while some people allow their challenges to handle them. For instance, there are people who would rather sit at a bar and attempt to "drink" their problems away, rather than spend quality "thinking" about a game plan that could help them overcome their problems. Have you ever noticed how the people who drink usually say, "I'm a social *drinker*?" When was the last time you heard someone say, "I'm a social *thinker*?" Think about it. Companies are *thinking* when they create the alcohol for people to buy and drink. There are people who have become alcoholics because they don't *think* they can stop drinking. *Thinking* before drinking has helped thousands of people stop the habit. If you drink alcoholic beverages, you don't need a *drink* to "think." If you have a problem *before* you drink, you will have the same problem before, during, and after you drink. Problems are challenges, and challenges can be conquered. If you have a personal problem, *drinking* won't give you the answers that you're seeking. "*Thinking*," instead of *drinking*, will give you the solution to overcome your personal challenges.

A friend of mine stopped drinking alcohol, simply from me asking her one question. The question I asked her was, "*Why* do you drink alcohol?" She told me that she drank to relax, and to celebrate her accomplishments. My comment to her was, "So, are you telling me, 'Every time you accomplish something and celebrate something, or need to relax, you are going to drink an alcoholic beverage?'" She stood speechless. Then, I asked her, "*Why* do you drink?" Her response was, "I *drink* because I'm used to people asking me to drink with them."

A few days later, after thinking about my question, "Why do you drink?" She called me, and said, "Skip, I thought about what you said. I've decided to stop drinking alcohol." The last time I talked with her, she told me that she was keeping her distance from alcoholic beverages.

One effective way to think is by "thinking" responsibly. Winners don't look for ways to *drink* their problems away. Winners look for ways to *think* about new solutions. Winners are looked upon as examples. As a winner, you are an example for others. You must stand up and be the best example that you can be. For instance, people are not going to come up to you, tap you on the shoulder, and say, "Excuse me, *you* are my example." But, you better believe someone is watching you from a distance. If you don't believe me, do something different, and watch how many people will look at you. For example, a child might not say, "Mommy or daddy, *you* are my example." However, the child is watching *you* to see "what" you're doing, and "how" you're doing it. Why? Because the child knows that *you* are his or her example.

As human beings, we are all examples. We learn through watching other people, and through our own personal experiences. There are millions of people around the world that love Oprah Winfrey, and the actor Will Smith because they are both great examples. Every time you see Oprah and Will Smith they present themselves in a manner that make people want to see and listen to them.

As a winner, you will need to become more than a responsible person, you will also need to step up and become a great example, and a responsible thinker. Cheers! I'll *think* to that.

23

THE WORRYING DOCTOR
WILL SEE YOU NOW

Why are you worrying yourself over unnecessary things?

The humorist Evan Esar observed, "Worrying is like a rocking chair; it gives you something to do, but it doesn't get you anywhere." There are people who don't live or enjoy their lives because they focus their thoughts on what others think or say about them. You can't stop people from thinking or talking about you, but you can always give them something to think and talk about.

One vital lesson I learned is that people are going to talk about you–if you like it or not. Regardless of what people say about you, you must create your own path, and stay focused on what you want to achieve. If you're always thinking about what people are saying about you, it will be harder to discover your own path in life, because you will be too worried about what people may think or say. Let people think and say whatever they want. Always keep in mind that you are the sole person with the correct answer to the questions that are lingering around in people's curious minds. For instance, people will think they know everything about you, but in actuality, you're the only person who knows everything about you. Couples may think they know "everything" about each other. However, there is at least <u>one</u> thing that one or both of them forgot to mention to each other. The next time you think someone is thinking or saying something negative about you, don't worry about it. Why would you worry about negativity, when you have more constructive thoughts to occupy your mind?

It's a doctor's job to help patients. However, some of the patients who make appointments to see the doctor are not physically or mentally ill. They are "worrying" ill. How many people do you know that *worry* about what others think and say about them? How many people do you know who *worry* about losing their job? How many people do you know who *worry* about if someone likes them or not? The bottom line: *Worrying will keep you from enjoying your own life.*

Are you going through life with a "What will people say" mentality? This usually occurs when you place the majority of your concentration on thinking about what people will say about you. As the renowned bestselling author Napoleon Hill asserted in *Think & Grow Rich,* "Too many people refuse to set high goals for themselves, or even neglect selecting a career, because they fear the criticism of relatives and 'friends' who may say, 'Don't aim so high, people will think you are crazy.'" What's crazy is letting someone talk you out of living and enjoying your own dreams. How successful do you think you will be if you're constantly worrying about what others think or say about you? Now, ask yourself, "How successful could I become once I stop worrying about what people think about me?"

You can eliminate peer pressure. In her book, *What You Think Of Me Is None Of My Business,* Terry Cole-Whittaker stated, "Virtually all of our problems are either caused or compounded by our obsessive need for acceptance and approval from other people." Who are you trying to receive approval from? Could it be from your parents? Friends? Boss or colleagues? To win, you must adopt the winners' attitude. Winners know every person in the world won't like them. This is why winners don't lose sleep when it comes to others talking about them. Most people will talk about you simply because they want to know more about you. Let people think and say whatever they want about you. At the end of the day, your focus should not be on what *people* say or think about you. Your focus should be on what *you* think and say about yourself. Remember, just because people are talking about you doesn't mean you have to listen to them.

As a winner, never let people, places, and things worry you. Place your mind on what you want to achieve, instead of negativity. When you place your focal point and actions on what you want to achieve, you won't have time to worry about what people say or think about you, because you will be too busy enjoying your life.

24

WAKE UP YOUR PURPOSE

Did you wake up your purpose or is it still asleep?

Winners start their day with a *purpose*. There are countless winners who have found their purpose in life. Some winners have discovered their purpose before others. There are people who wake up, and go to work because they think their job is their life purpose. Nevertheless, when they arrive to work, receive, and open up their paychecks, they quickly say, "What's the *purpose*?"

"To win daily, you must wake up with a purpose daily."

Every person has a purpose in life. Many people have discovered their purpose. Some people are still seeking their purpose. There are single mothers who work two and three jobs to take care of their children. There are firefighters who enter burning houses and buildings to save lives. There are teachers who dedicated themselves to educating students. There are various charities that have been established to research and develop innovative solutions to make a difference in the world. Why are they all committing themselves? Because they have all found their *purpose*. As a winner, your purpose is not always about *you*. Your purpose is always about something *bigger than you*. To win daily, you must wake up with a purpose daily. One reason people stay in bed is not because they are tired or lazy, but because they haven't discovered their purpose yet.

There is a calling within you that is ready to be displayed. You don't have to search inside your pockets, as though you're looking for coins to say, "I know that I have a purpose in here somewhere." If you haven't found your life's purpose yet, don't kick yourself, doubt yourself, or put yourself down. One thing you must understand about a purpose is that everyone's purpose is not the same. For example, your purpose may differ from my purpose, and my purpose may differ from your purpose. Likewise, your purpose could be more obvious, intense, and heartfelt than your parent's, friend's, spouse's, and/or next-door neighbor's purpose.

Renowned professional speaker and bestselling author, Dale Carnegie, declared in *How to Win Friends & Influence People*, "You can make more friends in two months by becoming interested in other people than you can in two years by trying to get other people interested in you." Rather than focusing all your attention on *yourself*, sometimes it's best to share the attention and focus on *others*. As human beings, our overall life purpose is to help others, and to live our life to the fullest. As winners, we have one common purpose in life and that is to "give." I'm not talking about *giving up or giving in*. I'm talking about "giving out." What is *giving out*? Giving out is when you maximize your potential, on a daily basis. Giving out is when you refuse to give up and give in. Giving out is when you help others succeed. Giving out is a form of giving back.

Do you remember when your parents told you to share your toys with the other kids in the sandbox? The same scenario applies today. You will need to share what you have with others (your time, ideas, energy, and support) by giving it out to others. Every success revolves around helping others. Ask yourself, "How can I contribute to helping others?" One effective way is by volunteering. When you volunteer your time and help others succeed, you will succeed as well. Whatever you decide to give, it doesn't have to be a lot. Simply, give what you do have or what you can afford to give to others. When you give and share what you have with others, you will discover your life's purpose. Winning is not about being selfish. Winning is about being unselfish. The people who win the most in life are the unselfish people, because they don't put emphasis on the individual winning, they focus on the whole team winning.

As a winner, start your day with a purpose. Commence to look for ways to serve and help others daily. The more people you help, the more you will wake up and fulfill your purpose.

25

MAKE YOUR OWN DECISIONS

Decisions, decisions, decisions; where art thou?

There are plenty of things that I love about life. One thing I love about life is that I'm able to make my own decisions. How many people do you know who make their *own* decisions? How many people do you know who have to ask others for permission before they make a decision?

I recall one particular client, who seemed to let everyone make his decisions for him. It was as if he didn't have a mind of his own. Every time I turned around, someone was making decisions for him. First up was my client's father, who didn't make one or two decisions, but made it his duty to make every decision for my client–all the way down to what he would eat for lunch. Next up was my client's wife, who was second-in-command of my client. Then, came my client's sisters. Lastly, were his friends. There were so many people making decisions for my client that it got to the point where his mind and body just shut down, until he had a nervous breakdown.

My client's inner world (his brain) became so tangled up with massive confusion that it made his mind and body befuddled and weak. As the leadership expert, author and speaker, John C. Maxwell stated in his book *The Difference Maker*, "You can make a decision to have a good attitude, but if you don't make plans to *manage* that decision every day, then you are likely to end up right back where you started." This is what happened to my client. He wasn't managing his own decisions, because everyone around him was making his decisions for him. There were so many people orchestrating his decisions for him that he forgot that he had his own mind and his own voice. It had literally reached the point that whenever someone made a suggestion, he just simply agreed with the person by saying, "Yes" or "Okay."

After witnessing how others took it upon themselves to make the decisions for my client, I intervened by politely pulling him aside away from everyone. Looking directly into his eyes, I asked my client, "Do you know the location of your brain?" Somewhat baffled by my question, he slowly said, "Yes." Then, I asked him, "Do you know the location of your mouth?" Still trying to figure out where I was going with my questions, he replied, "Yes." In conclusion, I said, "It's great that you know the location of your own brain and your own mouth. Now, it's time for you to start using both of them for yourself." As my client stood in front of me speechless, I stated, "You are a grown and highly intelligent person. Stop letting others make your decisions for you. Stand up and start using your own brain and your own mouth to make your own decisions."

I said the previous statement to my client because I had made my own decision. I had decided it was time for him to hear the truth. No one likes "yes" people around them. I know I don't. One reason I keep "yes" people at a distance is because if you always have "yes" people around you, you will never get the truth. The truth may hurt, but sometimes the truth is what you need to hear. A few weeks later, I called my client, and I noticed a gigantic difference in his demeanor. One of the main things that I quickly observed about him was his tonality. His voice was more confident. He had started speaking with authority, instead of whispering his words.

As a winner, you will need to make your own decisions. There is nothing wrong with asking questions. But, make sure that you are the ultimate decision-maker in your life. Nothing comes easy, so go ahead and make the tough decisions. Life is a series of endless decisions. Every moment of your life you have a decision to make. Not making a decision is still a decision. Will you decide to do the right thing or the wrong thing? The decision is yours. Keep in mind that it will be the choices you make (or refuse to make) that will make the difference in your life, relationships, finances, and victories.

26

PUT CONFIDENCE ON YOUR SHOULDERS

*If you had the opportunity to play in the Super Bowl,
which team would you play for: Fear or Confidence?*

There are various products that come with an instruction manual. For example, televisions, microwaves, cars, computers, and software programs are just a few items that come with an instruction manual. However, when it comes to our "self-confidence," an instruction manual doesn't inherently exist. We must create our own personal manuals to our own *self-confidence*.

As a winner, your self-confidence doesn't come from what people tell you. Your self-confidence comes from what YOU tell yourself. This is why it's called *self*-confidence. What we mentally tell ourselves either strengthens or weakens our self-confidence. There will always be negative people who will attempt to throw darts at your self-confidence. You must be confident enough to defend your own self-confidence.

Winners learn how to survive and succeed. When I launched my own company, people told me that I would fail. Also, several people tried to make me fail. In spite of the numerous encounters that I experienced along the way, I still survived and succeeded. One lesson I learned in life: people will try to deter you from your journey toward success. You must be strong enough to stay on your own journey until you succeed. How many people have tried to talk you out of something that you wanted to do? What did you do? Did you give up or did you keep going until you succeeded?

The author, Charles B. Newcomb stated, "There are always two voices sounding in our ears–the voice of fear and the voice of confidence. One is the clamor of the senses, the other is the whispering of the higher self." Don't be afraid to go beyond your fears. To succeed in anything, you must have confidence. Without confidence, you will encounter fear and become weak. Without confidence, you will perpetually doubt yourself. Without confidence, you will lose your direction and get sidetracked. Without confidence, you will derail yourself from winning. Bottom line: without confidence, you will keep yourself from succeeding.

"Fear is an internal bully that you can internally defeat."

As the renowned motivational speaker and author, Zig Ziglar once stated, "Confidence is going after Moby Dick in a rowboat and taking the tartar sauce with you." If you lack self-confidence, your fear will internally run you over. Fear is an internal bully that you can internally defeat. Bullies only push around the people that they know they can push around or intimidate. To become a winner, you must enhance your self-confidence and conquer your fears. You can overcome your fears. Fear is a reflection of what your mind believes. You can either step on your fears or let your fears step on you. The choice is yours. You can also use fear to your advantage. Some winners use their fear as leverage to help them succeed.

Infants usually cry when they need their diapers changed, need food and milk, and when they need attention. As adults, we are old enough to feed and change our own self-confidence. Speaking of confidence, if there were a fence in front of you, and the only way that you could get on the other side of the fence was to climb over the fence, would you climb over the fence? Your *fear* is your fence. Whatever you fear, you will need to mentally, emotionally, or physically climb over it. To reach your ultimate destination, you must be willing to overcome your fears. When you mentally and emotionally elevate your self-confidence, believe in yourself, and give your best effort, you will surmount your fears.

27

THE BALL CALLED LIFE

*If you had to live your entire life in 24 hours,
what would you do with every second?*

Winners succeed because they have learned the rules of life. To catch the *ball* in life, you first must understand what life is throwing at you. Every day many people drop the *ball*, simply because they were never taught how to catch the *ball*. Think about it. If you were never taught how to ride a bike, would you know how to ride a bike?

Of course, some of us would eventually learn how to ride a bike. However, today there are still numerous people who don't know how to ride a bike. It's not funny, however, it's real. The same scenario happens every day in life. On a daily basis, there are countless people who think, walk, and act "downward" because they were never taught how to lift their heads upward. They walk around calling themselves "failures," "losers," and "nobodies." Anyone who constantly thinks about failing or in a negative manner will have a very difficult time succeeding in life. It's not that they can't succeed, because they *can* succeed. The key question: do they want to change themselves, so that they *can* succeed? As a winner, what are you currently doing to make sure you *will* succeed?

Mahatma Gandhi, the eminent political and ideological leader of India, once said, "You must be the change you wish to see in the world." Since some people were never taught how to succeed, many of them have developed low self-esteem. In their minds, they are thinking, "I'll never succeed anyway, so why should I try?" If this thought has entered your mind, delete it. One reason you must put forth the effort to succeed is because you will double your odds of succeeding. A *little* effort is better than *no* effort. If you *don't* try, you will stay in a rut. If you *do* try, you will give yourself more opportunities to learn and succeed.

There are winners who went from poverty to power, from being unknown to becoming a household name. How did they do it? They started dreaming bigger and aiming higher. There are millions of people around the world who were never taught how to "succeed." They were only taught how to "survive." When you think bigger, you will find the light that will lead you to success. It was in the midst of my personal hardships that taught me how to survive and succeed. Although I was barely getting by living paycheck-to-paycheck, and living in negative environments, I knew that I could achieve more in my life. Instead of beating myself up, I looked for innovative ways to *lift* myself up. I started reading more books, meeting new people, and visiting new places. In the midst of the process, I became a stronger, creative and better person. In life, when you're going through hardships, you can either let your ship sink or fix your ship to keep it afloat.

Keep your eye on the ball. Life will throw you various *balls*–fastballs, curveballs and change ups–you must be ready for what life throws at you. When it comes to the *ball* of life, you don't have to be an athlete to have possession. You can simply be yourself. The key to success is to put the *ball* in play. We all have the same opportunities to succeed, when we learn how to catch the *ball* in life. What is the *ball*? The *ball* is receiving and continuing your education. The *ball* is improving yourself and your surroundings. The *ball* is being willing, ready and prepared to achieve more in your life. The *ball* is starting your own company, instead of waiting on someone else to hire and fire you. The *ball* is having an open-mind, instead of a closed-mind. The *ball* is learning and understanding who you are as a person, and having a sense of direction of what you want to achieve in your life.

As a winner, the *ball* is always on your court. You can run, pass, or drop your ball. The choice is yours. Now that you have the ball on your court and in your hands, what are you going to do with it?

28

MISTAKES ARE US

If you make a mistake, does that mean you failed?

If you took a survey on the number of people who have made a mistake in their lives, every person would raise their hand because all of us have made mistakes. Mistakes are a part of life. Mistakes are made when we don't know which way to go. Mistakes are made when we are in a hurry. Mistakes are made when we don't know what else to do. We make mistakes because mistakes are us. As humans, we are fallible. From every *mistake* that you make, there is a lesson for you to learn something new.

Within learning come mistakes. Success is a learning process, so there are bound to be mishaps. As human beings, we learn via our mistakes. There are some people who go through life dreading to make mistakes because they think making a mistake will devalue them. It's our mistakes that show and teach us how to succeed. When people say, "Don't reinvent the wheel" they forget to mention, "*Mistakes* made the wheel." As Glenn Dietzel, the author of *Author & Get Rich*, wrote, "You aren't reinventing the wheel, simply redesigning it."

In every scientific project, scientists have learned through experimenting, mistakes, and discovering better solutions. For example, it took the exceptional inventor and scientist Thomas Edison a thousand times before he succeeded, but he accomplished his mission. Thomas Edison is known for inventing the electric light bulb. He also holds 1,093 patents in the United States and in other countries. It's been said that Thomas Edison *failed* a thousand times before he succeeded. Did Thomas Edison really *fail*? Or did Thomas Edison make a thousand *mistakes*, which enabled him to succeed? When a reporter asked Thomas Edison, "How did it feel to fail 1,000 times?" Mr. Edison simply replied, "I didn't fail 1,000 times. The light bulb was an invention with 1,000 steps." Mistakes will occur on your journey, but you must keep moving forward on your journey.

Success is built from mistakes. The majority of every success is learned in the course of trial and error. Every winner learns how to succeed through his or her mistakes. If you tried to do something and it didn't work, so what, you made a mistake. Many of us beat ourselves up because we make blunders in our lives. If we never made *mistakes* in our lives, we would never learn how to grow nor would we discover new ways to improve ourselves. It's our *mistakes* that show us what we need to do in order for us to succeed. It's our *mistakes* that teach us how to think creatively. It's our *mistakes* that start the process for us to learn how to succeed. It's our *mistakes* that teach us how to make ourselves better. Overall, we grow and succeed by making *mistakes*. Every winner has made at least one error in his or her life. Moreover, every winner learns how to succeed through his or her mistakes. If you asked successful people how they succeeded, they would probably tell you that they succeeded by learning from their mistakes.

The author and psychologist, Henry C. Link once stated, "While one person hesitates because he feels inferior, the other is busy making mistakes and becoming superior." Winners succeed in life because they are never afraid to make mistakes. How many times have you heard someone say, "I would try it, but I don't want to fail?" Being afraid to make a mistake will keep you from advancing in your own life. If you're afraid to make a few mistakes in your life, you will have a very difficult time succeeding.

Making mistakes doesn't make you a failure. Making mistakes will teach you how to succeed. Never view your mistakes as failures. Look at your mistakes as your personal teachers because they will show you how to win. The next time you try something and it doesn't work, don't tell yourself "I failed." Simply tell yourself "I made a mistake." As a winner, remember, mistakes breed success. The more mistakes you make, the more you will learn. The more you learn, the more you will succeed.

29

THE RIGHT NOW PERSON

*If things are going wrong, what are you doing
to make things go right?*

Winners move with a sense of urgency. Winners refuse to wait, nor do they put things on the back burner. Winners know precisely what they want, and they find ways to get what they want. Instead of sitting around counting their fingers or talking about what they would like to achieve, winners take action toward what they want to achieve, and they don't stop until they achieve it.

As I began to write this sentence, I took a brief moment to look up, and I instantly noticed a bright green post-it sticky staring directly at me with the words, "NEVER STOP UNDERLINE{UNTIL} THE WORK IS DONE!" Yes, all of the words are capitalized, and the two words are specifically underlined. I wrote the previous words and placed it on my desk for a reason. The post-it sticky does more than remind me that I have work to do. It's also my personal mini billboard, which consistently reminds *my mind* that there is no time for procrastination.

Procrastination is a form of wasting time. Why would anyone want to procrastinate when there's an abundance of activities that one could do? Napoleon Hill, the author of *Think & Grow Rich* wrote, "Life is a checkerboard, and the player opposite you is time. If you hesitate before moving, or neglect to move promptly, your men will be wiped off the board by time. You are playing against a partner who will not tolerate indecision!" Successful people like Oprah Winfrey, Bill Gates, and Jeff Bezos (the founder and CEO of Amazon.com) reached success because they didn't procrastinate on what they wanted to achieve. Instead of procrastinating, they took immediate action to achieve their goals. They became "right now" people. If you were to ask them if they wasted time, they would probably tell you, "I am too busy to waste time." The reason they are busy is because they are taking action *right now*.

Life is moving in real-time, so why would you want to delay your actions until later? Why wait until tomorrow, when you can take action today? What do you want to achieve in your life? What are you doing to achieve it right now? Have you done any research via the Internet, read books, or asked achievers questions to see what is required for you to achieve your goals? Have you set your goals? Have you made any phone calls to schedule meetings with the achievers who can help you succeed? Wasting time is never on the to-do list of winners. The key to winning is to use your time productively. As a winner, you must continuously seek and discover new ways to use your time in a productive manner. Never waste your valuable time on unproductive tasks.

When your objective is to succeed, you must become a "right now" person. A "right now" person doesn't put things off until later. A "right now" person makes it a priority to take action *right now*. If something needs to be done, he or she immediately takes action to start and complete the task. To win, you must do the same. Whatever you want to achieve, start taking action toward it *right now!* A minor delay in your actions could make the difference between if you succeed or fail. When you become a "right now" person, you minimize failure in your life. Once you become a "right now" person, you won't have time to fail because your actions will keep you busy, which will enable you to accelerate your success.

As a winner, you can and will succeed once you start taking action toward what you want right now. Write out your goals. Focus on your most important goals. Start taking action toward your goals right now. Don't waste another second making excuses for why you *can't* succeed, because you *can* succeed. The moment you start taking action toward your goals, it will begin the momentum for you to achieve your goals. Every step that you take toward your goals will place you another step closer to achieving them. Keep moving toward your own goals. NOW is the perfect time to start taking action toward what you want to achieve. Once you become a "right now" person, you will begin to achieve your goals *right now!*

30

SEEKING SUCCESS

If success were your best friend, what nickname would you give it?

As human beings, we are all seeking something in our lives. Some of us are seeking relationships, love, and happiness. Some of us are seeking spiritual guidance. Some of us are seeking wealth. Some of us are seeking new ideas, new strategies, and new solutions. At the end of the day, we are all seeking something that will enable us to succeed. As a winner, what are you seeking?

It's usually the negative thinkers who always think and say, "Success is impossible." Positive thinkers are strong believers who think and say, "Success is possible." We are living in the 21st century where just about everything imaginable is *possible*. If you have a goal, dream or an idea, you can make it happen. I may wear many hats, but I always view myself as a *positive and possible* thinker. When I believe that I can achieve something, I take action to make it happen. You can succeed when you believe in yourself. The next time a negative thinker utters, "Success is impossible" to you, simply reply, "Pardon my optimistic language, but success is possible." It's not foreign to succeed. Success is universal, which means anyone, regardless of the person age, race, background, country or culture can succeed. There are millions of people who have traveled thousands of miles from various countries to live and enjoy *the American Dream*.

When you have a dream or a goal that you want to accomplish, you must be determined to do what it takes to achieve it. Success has your name on it. What will you do to succeed today? Sometimes you don't have to go far to succeed. When you want to succeed, you can find success in your own backyard, garage, or on your own kitchen table. Some of the world's most successful people started their own businesses in their own homes. For example, Steve Jobs, the founder of *Apple*, started his household name company inside of his parents' garage. Today, *Apple* is a household brand. We see the *Apple* logo and products around the world via iPhones, Mac computers, iPods, and iPads.

After looking around and seeing all the BIG apples on the tree, a baby apple asked one of the BIG apples, "What do I have to do to get BIG like you?" The BIG apple replied, "You must be willing to blossom." If you noticed, even the little apple is seeking success. Winners know success is possible. This is one of the main reasons why winners strive to win. Henry Wadsworth Longfellow, the creative poet, once stated, "Within ourselves are the seeds of triumph or defeat." One thing you need to understand about success: Success is limitless. There are no limits to success, which means you can succeed in anything that you put your mind to achieve. What would you like to achieve in your life? When you know *what* you want to accomplish, the key is to find ways to achieve it. Success is built through increments of improvements and achievements. The more you strive to *improve* yourself, the more you will succeed. The more you *achieve*, the more you will succeed.

There are times when you will need to plant your own success seeds in order for your own success to grow. Waiting on someone to come along to plant your success seeds for you is like waiting for the rain to come along, when the sun is shining bright without a cloud in the sky. Don't wait for your success to come to you. Take the initiative and make your own success happen. As a winner, *you* control the height and the width of your own success. What will your success measurements be today?

Like the Bible says, "Seek and you shall find." Start seeking within yourself for what you want to achieve. The moment you start looking within yourself, you will begin to discover various elements that will help you succeed. One effective way to succeed is to first know "what" you want to achieve in your life. When you know *what* you want to achieve, or have an idea about what you would like to accomplish, you will begin to expedite your achievements, which will enable you to succeed faster in your endeavors.

31

WINNERS GO BEYOND FAILURE

If you could win more than you failed, what would you do?

Seneca, the Roman philosopher, once said, "Admire those who attempt great things, even if they fail." Every winner has experienced defeat at least once. If you have failed at something, stand up, and shake it off. There is always more than one way to succeed, even if you have failed multiple times.

Winners get knocked down, but they refuse to stay down. Despite the amount of times winners get knocked down, they do whatever it takes to get back up. The musical group called *The Hours* recorded a song called "Ali In The Jungle." In the song, there is a line that goes, "Everybody gets knocked down. How quick are you going to get up?" If you fail at something, you have the choice to either stay down or get up. Which one will you choose? In order to become a winner, you must *get* up, instead of *give* up. Winners know there are no rewards if they give up–that's one reason why they refuse to quit. When you strive for something more valuable and bigger than yourself, you will find the strength to stand up. Stand up for your family, a cause, and/or your own dreams. When you stand up, you will stand above failing in life. Life and people will attempt to knock you down, but you must be resilient and stand back up.

Although Humpty Dumpty fell down, he never called himself a failure. Failure is on the other end of the seesaw, which can lift you up toward success. Your life may feel or look unbalanced at the moment. However, there are a variety of ways to add balance into your life. Eating breakfast in the morning to start your day will add balance to your life. As the *Wheaties* cereals slogan states, "The Breakfast of Champions." One effective way most winners add poise in their lives is by developing a positive attitude. How do they do that? By thinking positive. Winners know thinking positive is the food for success. When it comes to winning, I always say,

"Think like a winner, not like a failure." If you attempt something and it doesn't work that is not an indication that you're a failure. The only way to fail is to not try. Simply trying something and putting forth the effort will place you above failure. You are <u>NOT</u> a failure. YOU ARE A WINNER!

Every person experiences adversity, but it's the winners who refuse to lose. Winners constantly create and find ways to overcome their challenges. It's overcoming the challenges that transform ordinary people into extraordinary people. As a winner, you can overcome and break through your present challenges. You can change your life from ordinary to extraordinary. You can turn your rough roads into smooth roads. You can bounce back up when you get knocked down.

There are an abundance of creative things that you can achieve once you put forth the effort to achieve them. When you think positive and take action like a winner, anything is possible. Every winner doesn't succeed the first time around. Nevertheless, every winner keeps going until he or she succeeds. Winners recognize that persistence breeds success. Despite the obstacles or the length of their endeavors, winners constantly keep their focal point on what they want to achieve, until they succeed. You can always identify winners because they refuse to take their minds, energy, and actions off of what they want to achieve. Once winners know what they want to accomplish, they mentally, emotionally, and physically commit themselves to take unstoppable action to achieve their goals.

Winners don't dwell on where they failed. Winners look forward and concentrate on where they are going in life. When it comes to success, you will experience a few defeats on your journey. Remember, winners go beyond failure. As a winner, go the extra inch and yard, but don't quit. The next time you try something and it doesn't pan out the first time, don't panic or quit. Pick yourself up, revise your game plan, and try again. It will be your game plan, determination, enthusiasm, and persistence toward what you want to achieve that will drive you to win.

32

INVEST IN THE INVESTOR

How many steps does it take to reach success?

The teenager asked her father, "Dad, why am I financially broke?"

The father replied, "Maybe because you're spending too much of your time on unnecessary things."

The teenager said, "What unnecessary things are you talking about?"

The father stated, "Unnecessary things like spending too much time talking on the telephone with your friends about who is dating who." As he continued, "Sweetheart, if you want to become wealthy you will need to change your habits. Instead of wasting your time talking and texting on the phone, start spending more of your time learning how to accumulate wealth." In conclusion, the father told his daughter, "Start looking for ways to invest in yourself. One profitable way that you could start investing in yourself is by creating your own Internet business."

Time is a valuable asset. Invest your time wisely. Do you think the world-renowned investor, Warren Buffett look for ways to "waste" his time or look for ways to "invest" his money? When it comes to wealth, the more you educate yourself on how to invest in yourself, the wealthier you will become. It's never too late to learn, win, succeed, and prosper in life. Every moment is a new beginning to achieve more in your life. Whatever you accomplished yesterday, you can accomplish more today. Whatever you learned last week, you can learn more this week.

If *you* were an IPO (Initial Public Offering) stock, would you invest in yourself? The key to investing and winning is learning how to maximize what you already have. For example, if you had a dime in your pocket, you would look for ways to invest your dime, so it could give you twenty cents or a quarter return on your investment. Once you have a quarter, search for ways to transform your quarter into fifty cents. Once you have fifty cents, seek creative ways to turn your fifty cents into a dollar. Bottom line: Look for investment opportunities that will "double" your initial investment. This is one reason you hear the phrase, "Buy low. Sell high." You don't have to start big or have a lot of money to succeed. You can start small and still succeed. At the beginning, you might not know or have *everything* you need, but when you continue to learn how to work with what you have, eventually you will get more of the things you want and need.

Paying yourself first is one way to invest in yourself. The majority of us have heard the word "goals." However, many people have never heard of "financial goals." Financial goals are important because they will help you accumulate the amount of money that you want to earn per year. Having financial goals will enable you to setup your 401k, IRA for retirement, mutual funds, a trust fund for your family, and additional investments for forthcoming vacations.

Winners are not afraid to take risks. A *risk* to a winner is an investment. Winners constantly invest in themselves by taking calculated risks. They know that risks will give them more return on their investments. As a winner, start viewing and accepting yourself as a hot commodity, because you are a valuable person. Every day ask yourself, "How can I *invest* in myself today?" The more you invest in yourself, the more leverage you will have to become a valuable asset.

Thinking is FREE! It doesn't cost you anything to think BIGGER. As you begin to think bigger, keep in mind that investing in yourself doesn't only pertain to money. As a winner, there is always more than just one way to *invest* in yourself. You can *invest* in yourself in a variety of ways. You can *invest* in books to learn how to improve yourself. You can *invest* in yourself by joining a fitness center to workout or by taking a walk in your community. You can *invest* in yourself by spending quality time with yourself via a self-appointment. Your mind, time, and ideas are worth a fortune. Start investing in your own ideas. When you *don't* invest in yourself, you become your own liability. When you *do* invest in yourself, you become your own asset.

33

CONDITION YOURSELF FOR SUCCESS

*What are you doing to prepare yourself
for your forthcoming success?*

As a winner, keep in mind that you can physically improve and change your own life. Recently, a young lady told me how someone didn't like her. I think we have all experienced what she was going through at least once in our lives. My response to her was, "You can't please everyone." Although you can't please every person that you meet, you can condition yourself for success.

Winners are constantly conditioning themselves for success. There is not a day that goes by that winners aren't doing at least one thing to make themselves better. I recall a seminar that I attended in Baltimore, Maryland. There were various inspirational speakers on the stage – Former U.S. Army General and Secretary of State Colin Powell, the Baltimore Ravens offensive lineman, which the movie *The Blind Side* was based on Michael Oher, and the 8-times 2008 Olympic Gold Medal winner, Michael Phelps – who shared their success stories with the audience. All of the speakers told compelling stories. However, Michael Phelps' conditioning for his success captured my attention. Michael Phelps described how he conditioned himself *every* day – 365 days – for over five years to win his 8-gold medals. He stated, "While other swimmers took the weekends off to relax, I trained seven days a week." Michael Phelps is a winner because he continuously trains and conditions his mind and body for success.

To win, you must condition yourself for success. If you never condition yourself for success, how do you think you will succeed? If you are affiliating yourself with negative thinkers, how do you expect to win in your endeavors? If you are sitting around at a friend's house playing video games all-day with your feet kicked up, more than you're taking physical action toward your goals, how do you expect to achieve your goals? You will achieve more, once you start conditioning your mind with a vision of yourself succeeding. You will begin to achieve more, once you start following through and taking action toward your goals. As a winner, you will need to condition your mind to believe in yourself and what you want to achieve. Rather than doubting and putting yourself down, start visualizing your forthcoming success. Instead of procrastinating and wasting time, start challenging yourself to accomplish more in your life.

Success is not made only for one person, a few people, or exclusively for the elite. Success is made for the people who take action to succeed in their lives. In other words, success is available to you, and every person who wants to succeed and win in his or her life. As I've stated on a few occasions, "If you know your own name, you can succeed."

Your entire life starts with *you*. Every success starts with how *you* condition yourself. Are you conditioning yourself with a negative mind and laziness? Or are you conditioning yourself with an optimistic mind and unstoppable action? The four most effective ways to condition yourself for success are:

1. Know what you want to achieve.
2. Believe in yourself.
3. Write out your game plan.
4. Take unstoppable action.

Most people don't succeed because they never discover what they want to achieve in their own lives. Winners know what they want to accomplish. As a winner, when you know what you want to achieve, you will succeed faster, because you will be halfway toward achieving it. Winners always believe in themselves. The more you believe in yourself, the more you will build your confidence to achieve more. Write out your game plan. Take action toward your game plan daily.

34

GET READY FOR WHAT YOU ASKED FOR

You asked for it, but are you ready for it?

As human beings, we have our own unique ways that we view ourselves. Some of us see ourselves as *average*. Some of us picture ourselves as *extraordinary*. Winners always view themselves as *the best!* How do you envision yourself? Do you see yourself as average, extraordinary, or the best?

An effective way to produce and receive quality results starts with how you mentally prepare yourself. Using the words, "I am…" is one way that will enable you to create your own personal value. The "I am…" concept will consist of you writing down the internal vision of how you see yourself. The following are the exact words that I personally use to empower myself to excel in my life:

- I am young.
- I am fun.
- I am energetic.
- I am healthy.
- I am productive.
- I am creative.
- I am passionate.

- I am ambitious.
- I am somebody.
- I am unstoppable.
- I am a winner.
- I am the best.

At the top of a piece of paper, write the words, "I am…" You can use this for every aspect in your personal and professional life. For example, you could say, "I am a loving mother/father." "I am a magnificent wife/husband." "I am beautiful." "I am sexy." "I am a passionate lover." "I am a confident person." "I am the best." "I am open-minded." Start your own "I am…" list today.

Success and winning is simple once you discover the right and effective format to use. Here is an easy format that will help you win: Think and select *positive words* that will describe you and empower you daily (Ex. "I am electrifying"). After selecting the words that you want to use, begin to repeat the "I am..." words to yourself out loud and/or silently. If the words you selected don't empower or energize you, change the words, until you find the right and effective words that will move you and ignite your internal energy into physical action.

"Preparation will prepare you for your forthcoming rewards."

Winners know preparation is a requirement for success. Preparation will prepare you for your forthcoming rewards. When you ask for something, you must be ready to receive it. Be specific about what you ask for. Some people ask for more money, without knowing *exactly* how much more money they want. For example, a friend told me that someone asked her for some money, so she gave the person a quarter. It might sound cruel to you, but the person never said *exactly* how much money he really wanted. We receive what we ask for. If you're not ready for what you asked for, you will either prolong its arrival, or you won't receive it.

The eminent author, Emmet Fox, asserted, "Be careful what you wish for because you're liable to get it!" Have you prepared yourself for what you asked for? Or are you procrastinating? Procrastination is not a game plan, nor will it prepare you for victory. Procrastination is *exactly* what it says, "procrastination." Nothing gets accomplished when you procrastinate. You will accomplish more when you prepare and take action. As a winner, you must prepare yourself for what you want to achieve. If you want to travel, have you already packed your bags for the trip? If you want to start your own business, have you selected the name for your company? If you want to be a singer, have you started taking singing lessons? If you want to become an actor or actress, have you started taking acting classes? As the Boy Scout motto states, "Be prepared." When you're *specific and prepared* for what you asked for, you will get what you asked for.

35

IS IT FRIDAY YET?

*Why do we applaud Friday more than Monday,
when both days are in the same week?*

When there are a multitude of opportunities to enjoy life, why would you want to have an *average* day, when you can have an *extraordinary* day? On a weekly basis, many of us look forward to Friday, so we can simply say, "Thank God it's Friday." The best day of the week is TODAY!

There is a famous restaurant called "T. G. I. Friday's." Though many of us live for Fridays, when was the first or last time you have seen an eatery called "T. G. I. *Monday's*?" When was the last time you heard someone say, "Thank God it's Monday?" Every day more and more people are growing accustom to waiting for "Friday" just to live and enjoy their lives. Monday through Thursday, I see and hear people complaining about their lives, jobs, and finances as though they can't make it another day. But, as soon as Friday arrives, they quickly forget about what they were complaining about as they instantly become enthusiastic and fully energized.

Have you ever noticed when you ask someone how he or she are doing on Friday, they quickly say, "It's Friday" with a smile on their face? But, when you ask them how they are doing on a Monday, they slowly say with a grimace, "It's Monday." Are you a Monday or a Friday person? If you are a Friday person, what if *every* day were Friday, how would you live your life? The part most of us don't realize is that Friday is a regular day like every day of the week. If you live for Friday, why not live *every* day like it's Friday? Why enjoy one day, when you can enjoy every day? If Friday is your favorite day of the week, make *every* day your favorite day. Regardless of what day it may be, live your life like it's Friday.

What is your peak performance day? After asking various people the previous question, the response I heard the most was Wednesday and Friday. Why? Wednesday is considered "over the hump day" and Friday is viewed as "the beginning of the weekend." Do you wait until Wednesday and/or Friday to give your best effort? If so, what are you doing with the other days? Make *every* day your best, not just one or two days per week.

Winners enjoy Friday's like everyone else. Nevertheless, winners know success doesn't occur only on Friday. Winners know success is a *daily* issue. This is one reason why winners challenge themselves every day to exceed what they have already achieved. If you recall in the *Condition Yourself For Success* chapter, I mentioned how the 8-times 2008 Olympic Gold Medal winner, Michael Phelps conditioned himself by practicing 365 days, while his competitors took the weekends off. It wasn't a coincidence that Michael Phelps won 8 Olympic Gold medals. Michael Phelps won because he trained very hard and worked diligently every single day. He didn't train just *one or two days* a week. He trained *every* day. If you're going to be a winner, be a "full-time" winner, not a "part-time" winner. Stop half-stepping through life. Start taking whole steps. Go full steam ahead. There is nothing wrong with enjoying the weekend, but make sure you handle your business first.

Winners are willing to do what others are *afraid* to do, and what others *refuse* to do. As a winner, make every day your Friday. Condition yourself to start taking "Friday" action steps daily. Every day, put the pep in your step like it's Friday. Every day, put a smile on your face like it's Friday. Everyday, wave and talk to people like it's Friday. Every day, laugh like it's Friday. When you think, feel, talk, walk, and act like it's Friday, you will enjoy every day as though it is Friday. Once you make every day your best day, you won't have to ask, "Is it Friday yet?" When you make every day your Friday, you will have others asking you, "Is it Friday yet?" because they will notice your enthusiasm, while you're enjoying every day of your life.

36

WHAT'S NEXT?

How does it feel to walk inside of your own dreams daily?

If you don't know what you want to achieve in your life, start asking yourself questions that will open your mind's eye to new possibilities. Questions like, "What do I want to achieve in my life?" and "What's next?" will launch your mind into "creative thinking" mode. Once you have an open-mindset, your triumphs will be endless.

Winners are always asking questions. Why? Because winners realize they don't know everything, but by asking themselves and others questions, they will receive new answers that will produce new results. Winners are constantly asking themselves "What's next?" because they are always looking for new ways to achieve more in their lives. Asking yourself a single question like, "What's next?" will not only open your mind to new ideas and new solutions, it will also lead you to new people and new paths that will show you how to succeed.

When you ask yourself, "What's next?" it's as if you're asking yourself, "How can I make another prosperous step in my life?" Two of the best ways to prosper is by asking questions and through achievements. The more questions you ask, the more you will learn. The more you achieve, the more you will prosper. I have achieved many things in my life, simply because I'm constantly looking for new ways to succeed. Asking questions is one secret that has helped me succeed. I am perpetually asking myself, "What's next?" because I know there is always room for improvement. When you ask yourself, "What's next?" it will keep your mind churning to think bigger, which will enable you to become more creative.

Success is built from increments of action, achievements and persistence. If you never strive to achieve something, you will keep yourself from succeeding. An effective way to win is to take action. Every winner knows that luck is built from his or her actions, achievements and persistence. How can you win and accomplish more? You can start by asking yourself, "What's next?" For instance, ask yourself, "What's the *next* thing that I need to do to achieve my goals?" Start asking yourself, "What's the *next* step that I need to take to fulfill my dreams?" There is nothing wrong with thinking two steps ahead, even if you're still standing at the starting line. Winners think ahead, but they also *plan* ahead, so they will be prepared once they cross the starting line.

What is your *next* adventure? If you've started a new project, what's the *next* step that you could take to enhance it or complete it? The more you ask yourself, "What's next?" the more you will discover innovative ways to succeed, which will also give you more opportunities to win. Every winner knows what's next on his or her to-do list. This is one reason why winners set goals for themselves. Once they accomplish their goals, they strive to achieve their *next* goals. It's the achievements that drive winners to prevail. It's not hard to succeed, when you know what your next move will be. When you know your next step, not only will you give yourself an advantage, you will continuously build your own success. There are an abundance of things you can achieve in your life, once you start asking yourself better questions.

As a winner, what will you achieve *next*? Take a moment to think about the previous question. This is one reason why setting goals for yourself is vital, because the more you achieve your goals, the more you will continue to elevate yourself to the "next" level. Do you know what's next on your achievement list? If you don't know what's next on your list, start looking for new adventures that you could add to your list of achievements. Create your own *next* steps. Strive to accomplish between one through five tasks daily. As you complete each task, ask yourself, "What's next?" This concept will help you achieve more tasks faster. Moreover, it will boost your momentum to achieve your next milestone.

37

GIVE 1000%

Why give only 100%, when you have the opportunity to give more?

How many times have you heard someone say, "I give a 100%?" There are some people who tend to stretch themselves a bit by saying, "I give 110%." Then we have an array of people who say, "I give 210%." Out of all the percentages that I've heard, I've only heard a handful of people say, "I give a 1000%." Winners give a 1000%.

A few years ago, I was a participant in a well-known organization. While participating, I was matched up with a mentor. However, my mentor's thinking was too small for me. For instance, one day while talking to my assigned mentor, I said, "My goal is to give a thousand percent." His response startled me. He replied, "Nobody gives 1000% because the average person will only think up to 100 to 150%." I didn't agree with his statement, so I questioned it. The inquiry that I made to my mentor was, "If the average person had a choice to select $100 or $1,000, which amount do you think he or she would pick?" After my question, he became speechless. From my observation, I've always believed that $1,000 was more, and a better financial choice than $100. As a winner, why would you shortchange yourself when you can have the whole dollar?

Have you ever noticed how some people don't want to be called "average," but they continue to do *average* things on a daily basis? Average things consist of complaining, making excuses, blaming others, and getting frustrated, due to unwanted results. Average people complain and blame others when things are not moving fast enough for them, or when things are not going as planned in their lives. Though average people want extraordinary results, most average people will do average things just to receive minimum and average results.

Winners go beyond the average. An average person only puts forth a small percent of effort and hope that he or she will win. Winners refuse to lose. This is one reason why winners constantly work harder than everyone else. Winners may wear many hats, but they don't hang their hats on mediocre. While the average people are hoping to win, winners are working harder to improve themselves, so they can produce better results to win. When your goal is to be the best, you must be willing to put in the work that will continuously advance your progress and performance to new levels. As a winner, you may have to make a few sacrifices on your journey to reach your destination. Winners understand that making a few sacrifices comes with the territory. Making sacrifices is one key distinction that separates the winners from the average.

Average people grow *complacent* with their achievements, so they settle for what they have already achieved. Winners are *consistent*, so they never settle for what they have already achieved mainly because they know they can outdo what they have accomplished. As a winner, you are not average; you are extraordinary! Start setting higher standards for yourself and the people that you surround yourself with. Don't settle for what you have already achieved. You have the opportunity to achieve anything that you put your mind to, so strive to accomplish more in your life. Extend yourself mentally, emotionally and physically to perform at 1000%. At times it will seem as though no one is noticing your actions, but the more you give your best performance, the more it will make you stand out from the crowd.

As a winner, you must become determined to soar beyond the average. Refuse to settle for average results. Always strive for the best results. Remember, it will be your best results that will enhance your success. Start giving 1000% daily. Every day write down 5 tasks (goals) you will achieve. Prioritize each task from the most important to the least important. Take action to achieve all 5 tasks–starting with the most important task first. Every task you achieve is worth 200%. Your goal is to achieve all 5 tasks. After achieving all 5 tasks you will notice the completion of your achievements will accumulate into 1000% (ex. 200% x 5 tasks.)

38

THE ULTIMATE FOCAL POINT

What are you presently focusing on in your life?

There are an abundance of streets and highways throughout the world. If you don't know where you're going or if you aren't focused enough, you will definitely get lost along the way without reaching your destination.

If you could travel anywhere in the world where would you go? The law of attraction states, "What you focus on you will attract." In order to attract what you want, you will need to start focusing on what you want. What are you currently focusing on in your life? Are you focusing on what *you* want to achieve? Or are you focusing on what *others* want you to achieve? Every person wants to achieve something, and every person can achieve something. Most winners focus eighty percent of their minds, time, and actions on what they want to achieve. How do you think Oprah Winfrey and Donald Trump succeeded? They placed their focal point on what *they* wanted to achieve.

Every success starts with a focal point. The starting line to every focal point begins with having something to focus on. This is one reason why winners write down their goals, because having goals gives them the opportunity to focus on what they are out to accomplish. Aiming for achievement is a goal within itself. What do you want to achieve in your life? What do you want to achieve today? Tomorrow? Next week? Next year? Ten years from today? Having a focal point will keep you on track to achieve your goals, ideas, and dreams. When you know what you want to achieve, it will be easier for you to get focused.

Vince Lombardi, the legendary Hall of Fame NFL head coach of the Green Bay Packers, once stated, "Obstacles are what you see when you take your eyes off the goal." One key to victory is to "stay" focused. Winners are focused and action-oriented. When setbacks and obstacles appear on your path, don't allow them to sidetrack you. If you're not focused, it's easy to get distracted by people, places and things. When your objective is to win, you must stay focused. There will be people who attempt to deter you by wasting your time. Don't fall into their distraction trap. Most people get sidetracked and kicked off course, due to the lack of their focus. Without something to focus on, you will get sidetracked. If you get sidetracked, get refocused, and get back on track.

Every goal and dream encounters a challenge. For example, people will challenge your dreams by telling you, "Your dreams are too big" or "You will never succeed." It doesn't matter if you're homeless, jobless, or the richest person in the world–it's always your responsibility to live and enjoy your own dreams.

When it comes to focusing, concentration and discipline go hand in hand. Discipline is needed to stay focused. Lack of discipline will allow distractions to interrupt your concentration if you're not fully focused. When you are extremely focused on what you want to achieve, your mind, actions, and determination will refuse to allow anything or anyone to interfere or distract you from achieving your goals.

As a winner, you must get focused and stay focused. One way to discover your focal point is by creating your own focal point. Regardless if you're living paycheck-to-paycheck, start focusing on the bigger picture. Dream bigger. Think bigger. Start taking bigger action steps. What is your vision of success? Are you mentally and physically moving toward your vision of success? Remember the law of attraction. Keep your mind and actions focused on what you want to achieve. Whatever you're presently going through in your life, you can overcome your challenges. It will be your focus and actions, sprinkled with persistence that will enable you to win. Get focused, stay focused, and take action toward achieving your goals, dreams, and ideas.

39

LEAD THE WAY

As a winner, what are you doing to lead others?

Many of us have heard the phrase, "In order to become a good *leader*, you must become a good follower." That's true to a certain degree. There is a big difference between *studying the leader* to become a leader, versus *staying a follower* just to say, "I know the leader." There are people who are always striving to *follow* the leader, which always keep them behind the leader. The secret to becoming a leader is to "study" the leader. In other words, become a student of the leader.

When I was in the United States Marine Corps, I was taught valuable leadership skills that have continuously helped me succeed. Leadership is a skill that we all have as human beings, however, not all of us were shown how to step up and apply our own leadership skills.

Growing up as an only child, without a father, I was never properly taught leadership skills. It was during my enlistment in the United States Marine Corps, when I was first introduced to what the word "leadership" really meant. As I learned how to improve my leadership skills, I discovered that as a leader and as a winner, you must be willing to make your own rules to win. In life, there will be times when you will need to make your own rules. If you noticed, I did <u>not</u> say, "Break laws, break rules, or hurt someone." However, I did say, "Make Your Own Rules!"

A *leader* is someone who leads, and makes the rules. A *follower* is someone who follows, and follows all the rules. Which one are you? Are you a leader or a follower? If you're a follower go ahead and allow everyone to lead you. If you're a leader, step up, and start leading. It's the people who are willing to step up as leaders that usually have the most fun. It's the leaders who say, "I will no longer deny myself from being the best person that I can be."

Every day leaders tell themselves, "I will do my best to lead and show others how to produce better results."

As a winner, your personal triumphs will depend on how well you lead yourself and others. Winners succeed via their leadership skills. Many people fail in life because they were never taught how to stand up as leaders. Yes, we were taught how to follow others. Yes, we were taught how to follow directions. Yes, we were taught how to work for others. However, out of everything that we were taught in our lives, how many of us were taught how to step up as a leader? How are your *leadership* skills? What are you doing to improve yourself and your leadership skills? When was the last time you told yourself, "I am a *leader*?" How many times have you told yourself, "I will strive to become an *entrepreneur*, more than an employee?" When you woke up this morning, did you tell yourself, "I will take the *lead* today?"

A few days ago I noticed a bumper sticker that said, "Lead, Follow, or Get Out of The Way," which reminded me that leadership is almost like NASCAR racing. For example, if you notice, at the beginning of each race, all the cars follow the pace car. Then once the pace car moves out of the way, all the drivers of their own cars compete to "take the lead" to win the race.

There is a leader within you that is ready to lead. In his book, *Developing The Leader Within You*, the leadership expert and author, John C. Maxwell wrote, "Your leadership skills determine the level of your success, and the success of those who work around you." Leadership is about stepping up, not stepping down. Leadership is about helping others succeed. Leadership is about bringing out the best in others. Leadership is showing people that you do care what happens. Leadership is about believing in others when they might not believe in themselves. Mr. Maxwell was correct when he stated, "Everything rises and falls on leadership."

As a winner, step up and lead by example. Become a leader. Seek the clues that have helped other leaders prevail. There are plenty of leaders throughout the world. Select 1 to 5 leaders or inspirational influencers whom you admire. Study their leadership qualities. Choose the qualities that work best for you. Then apply what you have learned from the leaders whom you studied.

40

THE PERSONAL SURVEY

If you took a personal inventory on yourself,
what would you discover?

Everything you want to achieve starts in the midst of your own unique and creative mind. Once you understand that your mind is the compass to your own success, you will begin to point yourself in the right direction to arrive at your destination.

On the road to success, winners usually take a personal survey on themselves. Their personal survey usually entails a series of personal questions, which only they can answer themselves. For example, on their personal survey, winners ask themselves, "Do I have a *positive* or *negative* attitude?" If they have a positive attitude, they say, "check." They ask themselves, "Am I *focused* or *unfocused* on what I want to achieve?" If they are focused, they say, "check." Then they ask themselves, "Am I taking *productive* actions or *unproductive* actions in my life?" If they are taking productive actions, they say, "check." The number one question that most winners ask themselves, "Am I surrounding myself with the *right* people or the *wrong* people?" If they have the wrong people around them, they replace all of the wrong people, until they surround themselves with all the right people. Once they have all the right people around them, they go back to their personal survey, and check their list.

One reason most companies conduct surveys is to get a better understanding of what their customers like and dislike. Once companies discover what their customers like and want–they start producing and improving their products and/or services, so they can fulfill their customers' needs. Customer satisfaction is essential to making a business successful. Winners are always seeking innovative ways to double and triple their productivity. One benefit to conducting a personal survey is that it will give you the opportunity to research and discover new ways to improve yourself, so you can produce better, faster, and premium results.

Is it time for you to conduct a personal survey? This should be a daily event. Take a few minutes to spend some quality time alone with yourself – without distractions – so you can take a personal survey on yourself. A personal survey will enable you to analyze what is working and what isn't working for you. Moreover, you could view your personal survey as taking inventory on yourself. When was the last time you took an inventory on yourself? For instance, what is missing from your life? What do you need to add or replace in your life? What are you doing to get a crystal clear understanding about yourself? What are your likes and dislikes? What are you doing to improve yourself? How much time are you spending on making yourself better? When was the last time you raised your standards? These are questions that only *you* can answer. Also, these are the questions that will enhance your productivity.

As a winner, you must always strive to win. While taking the personal survey on yourself, the first question on your survey should be, "Am I surrounding myself with the *right* people or the *wrong* people?" If you're surrounding yourself with the right people say, "check." The *right* people will help you win. The *wrong* people will help you lose. When your objective is to win, surround yourself with winners, not losers. Next, ask yourself, "Am I committing myself to *excellence* or committing myself to *making excuses*?" If you're committing yourself to excellence say, "check." Next, ask yourself, "Am I ready to succeed in my life?" If you're ready to succeed say, "check." If you're not ready to succeed, what's holding you back? Could it be because you are afraid to succeed? Could it be because you think you might fail? If you're not succeeding in your life, you are either telling yourself that you can't or you won't succeed, or you're doing something (or not doing something) that is keeping you from succeeding. Next, ask yourself, "Do I have a *positive* or *negative* attitude?" If you have a positive attitude say, "check." Conducting a personal survey will allow you to check and align your focus, actions, and productivity.

41

POSITIVE vs. NEGATIVE

Will you make positive or negative decisions today?

As a winner, you can never have enough "positive" thinking friends. It will be the *positive thinkers* who will help you elevate your success to the next level. It will be the *negative thinkers* who will try to make you miss the elevator to the next level. You become like the people that you surround yourself with, so associate yourself with the winners who will help you win.

It's very easy to be a *negative thinker*, because all you have to do is think negative and complain all day about what you dislike, and you will be among the top negative thinkers in the world. Someone once asked me, "Why would anyone want to affiliate themselves with the negative thinkers?" My response was, "Every negative thinker needs a positive thinking friend." Every negative thinker's biggest pet peeve is to allow a positive thinker to succeed. Instead of maximizing their own potential, negative thinkers would rather scheme up devious ways to demoralize someone else's potential, especially if the person is a positive thinker.

Wherever you go, there will always be at least one negative thinker in the vicinity. Negative thinkers are toxic and negative influencers. Negative thinkers want you to fail. This explains why they say negative comments to you. Pessimistic people will attempt to talk you out of what you want to achieve by uttering, "You can't or you won't succeed." Negative thinkers become concerned about you only when they think and feel that you're about to do something positive, or when you do something that might place you in front of or above them. Negative thinkers are always trying to conjure up a negative plan to make you fail. They will attempt to do whatever it takes to keep you from advancing in your life. Will you fall into their trap or will you avoid it?

As Dr. David Schwartz asserted in his book, *The Magic of Thinking Success*, "Gossip hurts the listener because it directs their attention toward negative suggestions." Pessimistic people will always tell you not to go for what you want to achieve, simply because they don't want to see you win, nor do they want to see you happy. In other words, negative thinkers don't want you to live and enjoy your own dreams, because they didn't live and enjoy their own dreams. If a negative thinker is not concerned about himself or herself, do you really think he or she will be concerned about you? The answer is obvious... NO!

Listen to the winners, instead of the naysayers. As a winner, you must continuously believe and tell yourself, "I can succeed" and "I will succeed." Don't allow someone else's negativity detour you from your own success. Stay focused and stay on your path. Winners don't quit. Winners prevail. On your journey, negative people will attempt to place detour signs on your paths. In spite of the amount of negativity that you may encounter, keep pressing forward to achieve your goals. Sometimes it's good to use other people negativity as your fuel to win. Like I always say, "Never give the doubters and negative thinkers the satisfaction by quitting. Succeed anyway." Put on your running shoes and keep chasing your dreams.

As a winner, get in the habit of distancing yourself from negative thinkers because they are negative influencers and unhealthy for your success. In order to excel, you must subtract the *negative* people out of your life, and start adding and multiplying the *positive* people into your life. Today is the perfect day to start removing the *negative* people, places, and things out of your life. The sooner you get in the habit of removing the negative people *out* of your life, the sooner you will begin to make more room for the positive thinkers to *enter* into your life. Remember, you can never have enough positive thinking friends. Positive thinkers are positive influencers. It will be the positive thinkers who will help you discover new solutions in the midst of your turmoil. When you surround yourself with positive thinkers, you're also surrounding yourself with positive winners.

42

THINK OUTSIDE THE SQUARE

Will you live your life inside of a circle, square, or triangle?

As a winner, one of the most effective ways to succeed is to think "outside" of the box, even if you created the box yourself. When it comes to thinking outside of the box, there will be people who will think and call your ideas outlandish. So what? Think beyond the box.

Every dream, goal, and new idea is usually first challenged with an impossible thought. Why? Simply, because it's brand new. Whenever something is brand new, people will always be skeptical because it's something they are not accustom to seeing or using. Trends are often launched from new ideas. Though people will be skeptical of your new ideas at the beginning, never let others' skepticism stop you from thinking outside your own box. Think BIG! Dream BIG! Start thinking bigger and beyond your original box of thoughts.

Speaking of thinking outside of the box, a great example would be Michael Dell. For example, when Michael Dell started his Dell computer company, he started it "inside" of a box called his dorm room. Inside of his dorm room, he built his computer in the shape of a box. Though Michael Dell started out selling computers. Today, the Dell company sells laptops, MP3 players, cameras, and plasma TVs. Michael Dell succeeded as an entrepreneur and became a billionaire because his company focused on extending itself outside of its own original box.

When you have an idea about what you want to achieve, place your mind on building on top of your idea. Once you build on top of your ideas, you will begin to physically create your own success. Think bigger than the box, instead of within the box. One advantage to thinking outside the box is that you never limit yourself. When you're constantly thinking outside of the box, you will continue to place yourself beyond the limits in front, beside, and around you.

When it comes to winning, there are no rules that state, "You must succeed in a specific way or in a particular order." In other words, you can choose the sequence in which you want to achieve your goals. For example, most authors write their books first. Then they try to get on the radio or TV, so they can get interviewed and promote their books. However, I didn't go that route. I did things differently. Actually, I did everything backwards. For instance, instead of writing my book first, I started my own self-help TV show called *The Skip Williams Show*. Once I launched my own TV show, I wrote my first book *Think Progress*. If you noticed, I didn't follow the typical format of most authors. I created my own path and took the road less traveled. If you noticed, I didn't think and stay inside the box. I thought outside of the box and took a different approach.

"Winners always push themselves beyond the limits."

Winners always push themselves beyond the limits. How often have you heard the phrase, "Push the envelope?" *Push the envelope* means pushing yourself beyond the limits. Focus on extending yourself and your ideas beyond the original box. While everyone else is looking, playing, and staying "inside" of the box – step your game up, and become the person who will look, play, and stay "outside" of the box. As I stated to one of my clients, "Success is not like a coloring book, where you have to stay *inside* the lines. When it comes to your success, you can go *outside* of the lines because sometimes that's when you will discover and have the most fun."

As a winner, never limit yourself to staying inside of a square, circle, or triangle. This will limit your mind, actions, results, wealth, and success. Stretch your imagination beyond the boxes around you. The more you extend yourself beyond the box, the more you will broaden your opportunities to win more in your endeavors.

43

TELL YOUR OWN STORY

As the author of your life, how will you write your own life story?

Every person holds the pen, paper, and memories to his or her own life story. Although Helen Keller was blind and deaf, she told the world her story via her books and speeches. As a winner, will you tell your own life story? Or will you keep your mouth closed and hide behind a tree?

There are numerous books throughout the world on every topic imaginable from fiction, non-fiction, autobiographies, and all the way to how to communicate with your pets. However, when it comes to your life, you are the authentic author of your own book called "My Own Life." All of us have at least one unique "Once upon a time" story inside of us that we could share with others.

Authors write stories. Actors and actresses act out stories. Singers tell stories through their songs. Newspaper journalists write articles, which are stories about current events. What is your story? What adventure could you share with others? For example, when you woke up this morning, what did you do? When you went outside, what did you see, hear or experience? If you stayed inside, what did you learn? Overall, what have you accomplished thus far in your life?

The majority of all winners' stories start with their own personal triumphs and/or defeats. As a winner, what is your life story? What achievements could you share with others about how you succeeded? Like I always say, "Let the world know that you exist." One secret to success is letting people know that you exist. We have heard the phrase, "It's all about who you know." However, most people forget to add the second half, which says, "It's all about *who knows you*." For example, you may know Oprah Winfrey, but does Oprah know *you*? The more people that you let know you exist, the more successful you will become. This is one reason why celebrities hire publicists. They want to keep their fans in the loop of what they are currently doing, plus it broadens their name and existence in their industry while creating new fans worldwide.

An effective way to let others know that you exist is by sharing your story with them. You don't have to be a celebrity to share your story. You could simply be yourself. Once you tell your own story, people will show you how much they appreciate you and your story by requesting to know more about you. Once you achieve your goals, let others know how you accomplished them.

What would you like to achieve? Every day is another day to accomplish something new. There are successful people who started out financially broke, homeless, and without a high school diploma or college degree. Nonetheless, they refused to quit. Instead of quitting, they created astonishing ways to win in their lives. Some of them became entrepreneurs and launched their own businesses. A few received entry-level jobs and then worked their way to the top. The moral of the story: You always have the choice to either "hide" or "display" your own personal talents. Which one will you choose?

One of the main reasons most people don't succeed is because they fail to *follow through*. It's interesting how some people will follow others, yet fail to follow through on what they want to achieve in their own lives. Failure to follow through will not only cause regret, it will also keep you from winning and succeeding in your life. During the reading of your eulogy, do you want someone to read: "Here lies the best *follower* that I ever knew. He or she *followed others'* dreams, but forgot to *follow through* on his or her own dreams?"

Keep a journal. No one can tell your story better than you can. Share your wealth of success with others. You have read other people success stories. As a winner, what are you doing to convey your *own* success story? There are 365 days in a year, which means you should be able to write 365 pages in your journal about what took place in your life. One page a day is all it takes to tell your own story. Today is your day to narrate your own story. When you share your life story with others, you will do more than let them know you exist–you will also help others succeed.

44

MAKE IT HAPPEN

We can make cakes and cookies,
but what are we doing to make our lives better?

Are you "maximizing" or "reserving" your potential? If you're doing the latter, what are you reserving your potential for? Many of us waste our potential and lives away because we are waiting for something or someone to enter into our lives. There is a time and a place for everything. As a winner, the time is always right to make things happen in your life.

When you know what you want to achieve, and you're determined to accomplish it, even if you don't have the time, you will find and make time to diligently achieve it. How many people do you know who are just "waiting" in their lives? They are *waiting* for the right time. They are *waiting* for the right person to come along. They are *waiting* for the right job. There are people who are *waiting* in their lives, but they don't know what they are waiting on or whom they are waiting for. Nonetheless, they continue to go through their lives *waiting*.

The word, "waiting" is another word for "reserved." Instead of waiting, countless people have placed *reserved* signs on themselves. They may not be big, bright, shiny, and foreseeable for everyone to see, but some of us have placed reserved signs on ourselves, as we continue to wait for our reservations to show up in our lives. What if your reservations never show up? What will you do then? Will you continue to waste your time and life away for reservations that may never arrive? Or will you start making your own reservations to do more with your life?

One secret to winning is to *be productive.* Winners are productive individuals. Productive people win in life. Productive people constantly go beyond waiting. It's not that winners are impatient. It's just that they refuse to sit on their hind side and let life pass them by. Don't let your dreams, ideas, and life pass you by. The best way to succeed is to be productive. As a winner, you will need to be productive in your life. How productive are you? What are you doing, on a daily basis, to make every day a productive day? Yes, yesterday may have been a productive day for you, but what are you doing to make *today* productive? Will you sit on your laurels with your feet kicked up, and let the day pass you by? Or will you stand up and take advantage of today? The choice is yours. The latter will produce better results for you to win.

Following through on your thoughts and ideas are vital requirements to succeed. Most people don't succeed because they sit on their ideas. They have great ideas, but they never get up and take action toward their own ideas. In their minds, they either think their ideas won't work or that someone will laugh at them. Winners don't care who laugh at them. Winners believe in themselves and in their ideas so much that they take action toward their own ideas. Why? Because winners know they will eventually get the last laugh by turning their ideas into reality.

You have dreams. What are you doing to make them become a reality? You have goals. What are you doing to achieve them? You have a family. What are you doing to take care of them? You have a healthy body. What are you doing to keep your body healthy? You want to succeed. What are you doing to improve yourself? You want to elevate yourself to the next level. How many steps did you take toward your dreams today? Nothing happens by itself. Nor can someone live your life for you. In order to achieve what you want, you must take action and make it happen.

As a winner, are you *making* things happen, *watching* things happen, or *waiting* for things to happen? To win, you must "make" things happen. If you're waiting in your life, stop waiting. When your mission is to win, you can't wait for victory to come to you...YOU MUST MAKE IT HAPPEN! Get in the habit of challenging and maximizing your potential daily. Start telling yourself, "I will make my dreams, ideas, and goals happen!" Repeat it and say it with confidence. If you've always wanted your own personal motto, here is one for you: "MAKE IT HAPPEN!"

45

WINNING REQUIRES ACTION

How many hours do you work on improving yourself daily?

As I sit in my office thinking of a creative way to begin this chapter, I can't help but to notice how my mind feels as though it's running a marathon with ideas, while my fingers swiftly move from one letter to the next on the keyword of my laptop. My mind is being challenged. I know that if I don't get through this chapter it could delay the entire process of me completing this book. What should I do? (A) Should I *stop* typing, leaving my book unfinished? Or (B) should I *keep* typing, so I can finish and publish my book? Which <u>one</u> would you choose?

If you're still reading this book, you noticed I selected "B." Why? First of all, I'm not a quitter. Secondly, as a winner, I know action is required to succeed. Last, but not least, I wanted to show you that dreams do come true when you believe in yourself and take action toward your dreams.

There are various ways to win, but winners understand that "action" and "improvement" are the two core requirements to winning. Winners are discipline and action-oriented. Winners succeed because they discipline themselves to take action toward their goals, dreams, and ideas *every* day. Winners work hard and long hours on improving themselves daily. Winners are known for going the extra mile, while others dread going the extra inch. Winners constantly push themselves to improve their personal strengths and weaknesses. This is one distinction that makes most winners stand out from the mediocre crowd. While the mediocre crowd grows comfortable with producing *average* results, winners are never satisfied, until they produce *the best* results. This explains why winners relentlessly strive to improve themselves because they want to receive the best results. Winners know the most effective way to produce exceptional results is to work toward *the best* results. If you're not aiming toward "the best" results, what are you aiming toward daily?

Some people spend more time in the shower than they do on improving themselves. It's interesting how some people will work diligently *for* others, yet they forget to work diligently *on* themselves. There are winners who work full-time 9-to-5 jobs. Though they work a 9-to-5 job, they continue to find ways to work full-time on improving themselves while continuing to work toward what they want to achieve. Think about it. When was the last time you worked *40 hours plus overtime* on improving yourself and your life? When was the last time you did a *life* makeover? When you want to win, you must work on improving yourself daily. Without improvement, your life will remain the same. Do you want your life to remain the same or do you want to improve your life? What are you doing to improve yourself daily? Start working on improving your strengths and your weaknesses. Work on improving yourself, so you can build a bigger, brighter, and better future for yourself and your family.

All of us have at least <u>one</u> flaw somewhere in our lives. Winners constantly work on improving their flaws. The more you work on fixing your personal flaws, the more you will discover new opportunities to improve yourself. The more you improve yourself, the more you will win. Winning is not a *one* time event. Winning is not a *sometime* event. Winning is not an "I'll do it when I feel like it" event. Winning is a *daily* event. Winning is an "I'll keep pushing myself even when I don't feel like it" event. Winning is an "I'll never give up" event. You will accomplish more once you get in the habit of taking action. Action produces results. Action turn dreams into reality. Action conquers fear. Action breeds winners. To accomplish your goals, you must do more than just *think* about them–you must *take action* toward your goals.

As a winner, you must take action to win. No action. No glory! Although this book is called *Think & Win Big*, action is required. You must take action toward what you're *thinking* about. It will be your actions and improvements that will turn your goals and dreams into success. It's one thing to have an idea in your mind. It's another thing to take action toward your ideas daily.

46

DO IT ANYWAY

What do you really want to achieve in your life?

As I'm typing this book, a compelling thought entered my mind, which made me reminisce to when I used to work various dead end, 9-to-5 jobs. While working at one particular 9-to-5 job, I was contemplating leaving the job. One evening, while I was talking to a friend over the phone about my dreams and goals of becoming an entrepreneur, I received an eye-opening wake-up call. During our phone call, I spilled my heart out to her about becoming an entrepreneur, as she listened patiently. Then, after listening to what I had just told her, she quickly said, "Don't do it." I responded by saying, "Why not?" She replied, "Don't do it." After a minor pause in our conversation on the phone, she broke the ice by saying, "What is an entrepreneur?" I was stunned from her inquiry. Nonetheless, I explained to her the definition of an entrepreneur. Plus, I told her the advantages of it.

The moral of the previous story: When you want to achieve something, there will be people who will tell you not to go for your own dreams and goals, even if they don't understand your dreams and goals. This is why it's very important that you know what you want to achieve. Also, this is the main reason why you must focus your mind, beliefs, and actions on achieving your *own* goals and dreams. If you lack the focus on what you want to achieve, someone will attempt to talk you out of living and enjoying your own dreams and goals.

When you have your mind fully focused on what you want to achieve, it will be very difficult for someone to talk you out of what you have your mind, heart, and actions focused on. Winners succeed because they are focused and action-oriented. As a winner, you must get focused and become action-oriented. Whenever someone attempts to talk you out of something, and you have a gut feeling that you are doing the right thing, go with your gut feeling.

Never let people talk you out of what you want to achieve. When you know what you want to achieve, be like *Nike* and *Just Do It*. Don't contemplate, just do it! Don't focus on what "the people" might say – just do it! You're probably thinking, "But what if people laugh at me?" Just do it! One reason underachievers don't succeed is because they are afraid to get embarrassed. Don't be embarrassed to try something new. Don't be embarrassed to live and enjoy your own dreams. When your goal is to win, don't contemplate, simply put your best foot forward and go out and do it!

Success is achieved in increments, which means your small victories count too. It will be your small victories that will lead you to succeed. As Joe Henderson asserted in his *Complete Marathoner* book, "The seed of an idea grows into a goal, and from the goal sprouts a plan. The plan blossoms into training and finally matures as racing fitness." You might not be a marathon runner, but you're running toward something. All of us are running toward something in our lives. Many of us are running toward achieving our dreams and goals. Some of us are running on the streets, and running on treadmills to stay mentally and physically fit. Some are trying to run away from their past. A few of us are running around in circles. At the beginning and end, we are all running toward something. What are you running toward in your life?

If I achieved my goals and dreams, so can you. I started with nothing, but a dream and determination. I started at the bottom, and worked my way up to the top. I used to work for other companies; now I own my own company. Why am I telling you this? Because you can succeed too. When you believe in yourself enough to physically go for what you want to achieve in your life, you will eventually succeed. As I stated in my book *Think Progress*, "Don't cut down your tree before it grows." As a winner, start planting your success seeds. Then take action toward what you want to achieve, and you will make your success seeds grow into fruition.

47

GET YOUR POWER BACK

If you gave your power away, how are you going to get it back?

Winners have their own personal power to achieve whatever their heart's desire. Some people give away, lose, or misplace their power by lending it to others. It doesn't matter if you have lost or misplaced your personal power, you can find and regain your own personal power.

Many people don't succeed because they have voluntarily given their own power away. Whenever you give your power away, you will make it harder for yourself to win. It's one thing to look at the valuable things *outside* of ourselves, but many of us neglect to look at the valuable qualities *inside* of ourselves. As a human being and as a winner, always remember that you are a *valuable person*, and not a valueless liability.

"If you don't have a good view on the way your life is going, it may be time for you to stand up, so you can get a better view."

There are people who want to change their lives, however, they prolong their *decisions*, which continues to delay their actions for them to change their lives. In order for you to get your power back, you must become stronger. What is the most effective way to get your power back? One way is to start making better decisions. Yes, *decisions*! It will be your *decisions* that will indicate when you're doing something right or wrong. It will be your *decisions* that will produce your actions, results, and habits. It will be your *decision*, when you want to take your power back.

If you don't have a good view on the way your life is going, it may be time for you to stand up, so you can get a better view. When you lose or give away your personal power, you set yourself up to be easily intimidated or defeated. You're probably thinking or saying, "Nothing intimidates me." Many people will quickly utter that they don't get intimidated, simply because they know it will step on their ego. The word "ego" may be small, but to some people their ego is all they have because it defines their self-pride. Let's put a minor twist on the word "intimidation." Intimidation is a form of fear, embarrassment, reluctance, apprehension of change, lack of understanding, afraid to take risks, too worried about what others will say and think about you.

In my book *Think Progress*, I talk about how to give yourself a standing ovation. A standing ovation is about giving yourself credit and giving yourself a pat on the back. For instance, the next time you accomplish something give yourself credit for achieve it. I have on my desk a little red and silver button with the word "easy" on top of it, which I purchased from *Staples*. Every time I complete a task, I hit the red button on top, and it says, "That was easy." The moral of the story: It takes hard work to win, but once you start the process, winning will become a little easier for you. It may seem as though you have lost your power, but you can regain your power.

As a winner, you have all the power you need to win and achieve your goals. When you energize your personal power, you will refuse to let someone or something intimidate you. Winners refuse to get intimidated because they focus their minds and energy on winning. To win, you must do the same. Once you start viewing yourself as a winner, you will enhance your self-confidence to surpass intimidation. Eleanor Roosevelt, the First Lady of the 32nd President of the United States Franklin D. Roosevelt, once stated, "You gain strength, courage, and confidence by every experience in which you really stop and look fear in the face." If you've been looking for the perfect moment, now is the perfect time for you to stand up, look fear in the face, and take your power back!

48

SELF-IMPROVEMENT CREATES
THE BEST RESULTS

What are you willing to improve to make yourself the best?

How many times have you seen someone try to prove himself or herself to someone else? I think we all have seen it at least once. Some of us are still trying to prove ourselves to others. As I like to say, "When you want to 'prove' yourself, strive to 'improve' yourself." Self-improvement is one of the best-kept secrets of winners.

Every success begins with self-improvement. Winners know that self-improvement is the key to success. Self-improvement is a process, which produces endless success. One effective way most winners improve themselves is by keeping a journal. Keeping a journal is a very empowering process, because it will allow you to write down your ideas, goals and self-improvements. Writing down your goals and your improvements will help you visualize a plan of action. This is one of the main reasons why I always carry a mini notepad with me, because I am constantly setting new goals for myself to strive toward. Also, once I achieve my goals, I mark them off of my list. Another effective way that winners improve themselves is by writing down their goals on a little Post-it note, and posting them in places where they can see them daily. This is one of my favorites, because I have posted notes all around me. I even have Post-it notes in the bathroom on my mirrors, so as I wash my face, brush my teeth, and look in the mirror–I am reminded of my goals.

Another creative way to improve yourself is by writing down your goals, and carrying them with you everywhere you go. The actor, Jim Carrey is a great example of this. When Jim Carrey first got into acting, he always carried around with him a $10 million check, which he wrote to himself. Although he wasn't making $10 million at the time, Jim Carrey wrote down his goals, and took them with him everywhere he went. Today, Jim Carrey makes $20 million per movie.

The key to winning is to strive to improve yourself every day. Make *improvement* one of your goals. Write down the word *improvement*, on a piece of paper, and place it in a location where you can see it daily. When you have goals that you want to achieve, your goals will push you to improve yourself. Every winner didn't start out at the top of success. They had to constantly improve themselves, on a daily basis, until they achieved their goals. To achieve your goals, you must continuously improve yourself every day.

Every winner knows that self-improvement is a necessity to succeed. As a winner, if you're not striving to improve yourself, what are you doing with your life? Keep in mind there is always room for improvement. There are advantages to self-improvement. Self-improvement is about upgrading yourself and your surroundings. Self-improvement is about enhancing your imagination to see the bigger and brighter picture. Self-improvement is about challenging and pushing yourself beyond what you are used to doing. Self-improvement is about creating a better life for yourself and your family.

As a winner, your best always starts with *you*. You must be willing and courageous enough to want to improve yourself. The more you improve yourself, the better you will become as a person. The more you improve yourself, the more you will excel as a winner. Remember, the best results come from self-improvement. Self-improvement will not only advance you to the "next" level in your life, it will elevate you to the "best" level in your life.

49

GET IN THE HABIT

If you could produce your best results, would you make it a habit?

It's been said, "Human beings are creatures of habit." Our "habits" create our decisions and outcomes. Most of the things that we do in life, on a daily basis, are from the *habits* that we have mentally, emotionally, physically, spiritually, and financially conditioned ourselves to do.

Every person has a "habit," including winners. Yes, we take action because of our *decisions*. We also take action because of our "habits." There are specific things that we do daily without noticing our *habits*. For example, some people smoke cigarettes, which is a *habit*. Some people bite their fingernails, which is a *habit*. Millions of people drink coffee in the morning, which is a *habit*. Some of us wear our hair the same way every day, which is a *habit*. Many of us take the same route to work, which is a *habit*. The way we think about ourselves, about others, and about life is a *habit*. The people we surround ourselves with–good or bad–is a *habit*. We choose our habits; our habits don't choose us. Your personal *results* start with your personal "habits." Habits are learnable, which means if you have bad habits, you can learn how to develop *good* habits.

"We choose our habits; our habits don't choose us."

As a winner, open your mind to learn new habits. Winners create new habits that accumulate into success. Instead of creating bad habits that will deter them from winning, winners create good and effective patterns that will lead them to win. Winners know in order for victory to occur, they must get in the habit of doing whatever it takes to succeed. Remember, success has your name on it. What are you going to do today to succeed? Are you going to make excuses? Or are you going to make things happen?

Underachievers habitually make excuses. Overachievers habitually take responsibility for their actions and outcomes. The American scientist, educator, and inventor, George Washington Carver once said, "Ninety-nine percent of failures come from people who have the habit of making excuses." One reason most underachievers don't succeed or win in their lives is because they complain and make excuses. Complaining and making excuses won't produce effective results. If you complain and make excuses, those are bad habits. Bad habits breed bad results. Good habits breed good results. Get in the habit of doing whatever it takes to *avoid* complaining and making excuses.

Inside Emmet Fox book, *The 7 Day Mental Diet*, he introduces an innovative strategy to break habits and discipline your mindset within 7 days. I have read and personally used *The 7 Day Mental Diet*. At first, it sounds and seems easy. As you reach the third day that's when it becomes more challenging. Why? Because once you veer off the diet, you have to start all over until you're able to go for seven consecutive days. As Emmet Fox emphasized in his book, "The whole idea is to have seven days of unbroken mental discipline in order to get the mind definitely bent in a new direction once and for all." As a winner, are you up for *The 7 Day Mental Diet* challenge? If so, purchase the book, and give it a try.

As a winner, you must get in the "habit" of going the extra mile. Most people think winning is easy. However, it's the *habits* of winners that people overlook or never see that make it look easy. Winners practice hard and work long hours on developing their habits to succeed. Winners adopt the habit of excellence by giving their best performance daily. In order for you to excel, and become the best, you will need to develop the habit of maximizing your best effort. Get in the habit of using your time, and your talents more productively. While others are sleeping, get in the habit of waking up or staying up at least 30 to 60 minutes, so you can work toward achieving your goals, dreams, and ideas. When you develop good habits your victories will be endless.

50

THE SIMPLICITY OF LUCK

How simple can it be?

After all of the incredible achievements in history and around the world, there are people who continue to think it's impossible to succeed, due to the simplicity of success. Rather than looking at the simplicity of success, most people tell themselves, "It's either too hard or it's impossible to succeed." If others have succeeded, so can you.

Life is *simple*. We make it difficult. The Meyer's law says, "It is a simple task to make things complex, but a complex task to make them simple." Since we are talking about "simplicity," let's start with something simple. Hypothetically, let's say that you had one million pair of socks, and you priced each pair of your socks at one dollar. Yes, you read that correctly: Socks for $1. If you sold each pair of your socks for $1 to one million people, you would become a millionaire. You're probably thinking, "Yeah right, it can't be that easy." Like I said, "simplicity." If you're still a little skeptical about how easy it is for you to succeed, let's talk about some chewing gum. Yes, chewing gum. In 1893, William Wrigley Jr. started selling *Wrigley's Juicy Fruit and Wrigley's Spearmint* chewing gum, which he sold each pack of gum for under a dollar. Today, the *Wrigley's Spearmint and Juicy Fruit* gum idea is a billion dollar company, as the *Wrigley* company continues to sell its 5 sticks pack of chewing gum for less than 50 cents.

Do you still think it's impossible for you to succeed? You're probably saying the typical phrase, "He was lucky." Yes, Mr. Wrigley could have had a little luck on his side, at the beginning. However, he didn't depend entirely on luck to help him succeed. Mr. Wrigley was focused, determined, action and results-oriented. Mr. Wrigley succeeded because he placed his mental focal point on what he wanted to achieve. Most importantly, Mr. Wrigley took action, until he achieved his goals. As a winner, you must do the same.

> *"You might think luck doesn't run in your family or luck*
> *is not on your side, but when you believe in yourself,*
> *and take action toward what you want to achieve,*
> *you will eventually create your own luck."*

Winners believe the harder they work, the luckier they get. Achievers don't become winners by waiting on luck or coincidences. Achievers become winners through their exceptional actions and effective results. As the founder of *Virgin*, Sir Richard Branson, declared in *Screw It, Let's Do It: Lessons In Life*, "Success is more than luck. You have to believe in yourself and make it happen. That way others also believe in you." Winners are known to create their own luck. You might think luck doesn't run in your family or luck is not on your side, but when you believe in yourself, and take action toward what you want to achieve, you will eventually create your own luck. One thing you need to understand about winners: Winners don't place their luck on buying lottery tickets, because winners view *themselves*, as their own lottery jackpot ticket.

Winners refuse to wait for others to create their luck for them. The people who take action toward what they want to achieve are usually the winners who create their own luck. Entrepreneurs, leaders, and self-made millionaires and billionaires create their own luck.

As a winner, *you* must take action to create your own luck. *You* are your own lucky four-leaf clover when there is no grass in the vicinity. To succeed in anything, you must mentally, emotionally, and physically build up your confidence to take action toward what you want to achieve. As a winner, you must become determined to succeed. When you're determined to succeed, the word "impossible" doesn't exist. Once you start the momentum toward what you want to achieve, you will begin the process of creating your own luck.

51

UPGRADE YOURSELF

If you could upgrade anyone in the world, who would it be?

There are numerous levels in life. The best level is when you keep "upgrading" yourself to the next level. What are you doing to *upgrade* yourself to the next level? When it comes to *upgrading* yourself, aim higher! Although you may begin on the ground level, that doesn't mean you can't elevate to higher levels. As a winner, start putting elevators in your dreams. You can go from the ground floor to the penthouse level of success. You can go from being a mail clerk or secretary to becoming the CEO of the company. From one winner to another winner, "You *can* succeed."

One secret to success is to write down your dreams, and keep upgrading yourself, until you achieve them. As a kid, I always wanted to expand my personal horizons. I used to dream about success, traveling to new places, and meeting new people. As an adult, I get the opportunity to travel and meet new people. How did I do it? I wrote down my dreams, set them as my goals, and pursued them. I never stopped taking action toward my dreams, until I achieved my goals. As I reminisce, I truly believe that if I would have stayed in the same places, and continued to surround myself with the same people, I wouldn't have succeeded in life. If I didn't *upgrade* myself, my friends, my surroundings, my determination to succeed, and my mind with innovative knowledge, I would probably still be dreaming about my success.

Speaking of success, I enjoyed the story that a colleague named Pamela shared with me about how she upgraded, and pursued her dreams. Pamela told me that when she was 16 years old, she wrote, "I am a person with dreams to chase. I can't catch them if I stay in one place" on a piece of paper. Then she placed the piece of paper on the refrigerator in the kitchen. Although Pamela has grown-up and moved away from home, the same piece of paper is still posted on her family's kitchen fridge. Our dreams are always saying, "Catch me if you can."

As winners, we are all chasing our dreams. Many of us will catch our dreams. Some of us will continue chasing our dreams. Winners keep striving toward their dreams. For example, the Jamaican sprinter, and 3-times world and Olympic gold medalists, Usain Bolt knows about chasing his dreams. Usain Bolt is the world record and Olympic record holder in the 100 meters, 200 meters, and the 4 x 100 meters relay. Currently, Usain Bolt is the world's fastest man.

As a winner, dream bigger, and never stop chasing your dreams. Regardless of the situations you're currently going through, you can "upgrade" yourself to a better and more rewarding life. Make upgrading a part of your life. When you continue to upgrade yourself spiritually, mentally, emotionally, physically, and financially you will keep growing, winning, and succeeding.

Are you ready to *upgrad*e yourself? If you said, "yes," start by upgrading the people that you surround yourself with daily. Start associating with other winners. Upgrade your attitude. Upgrade your view on life. Upgrade your actions. Upgrade your outcomes. Upgrade your income. Upgrade your mind with optimistic thoughts. Upgrade your wardrobe. Upgrade your communication and people skills. Upgrade your self-esteem from low to high.

Every day is the best day to upgrade yourself. Winners take action to get better every day. An effective way to guarantee your own success is to keep upgrading your mind, actions, and results daily. There are 365 days in a year. Imagine if you improved yourself 1% per day, you would upgrade yourself 365% per year. It will be the little improvements you make every day that will make the big difference in your life and triumphs. When it comes to "victory," small victories count too. Small victories breed big victories. Winners understand big victories don't occur overnight. Moreover, winners know it will be the series of small victories that will eventually produce the big victories. As a winner, never miss a day to *improve* yourself. The more you *improve* yourself, on a daily basis, the more you will continue to "upgrade" yourself every day.

52

ASK QUESTIONS

How many questions did you ask today?

Asking questions is one of the most overlooked ways to win. How many people do you know who avoid asking questions? Have you ever noticed how some people refuse to ask someone a question because of their sensitive ego? They think asking questions will make them look stupid or weak, so they avoid asking questions. One advantage to asking questions is that you will receive your answers faster. Instead of mentally dwelling on something that you don't know, simply ask someone to assist you with the answers that you're seeking. If you don't know something, ask questions. It's not hard to succeed once you ask questions.

As the bestselling author Richard Bach, once stated, "The simplest questions are the most profound. Where were you born? Where is your home? Where are you going? What are you doing? Think about these once in a while and watch your answers change." Winners know there is always room for change. Winners are always seeking innovative ways to change, improve, reinvent, and upgrade themselves. This is one reason why winners are relentlessly asking various questions, because they know solutions are only a few questions away. Likewise, winners know asking questions is the fast track to winning.

Have you ever noticed how some people see the "flaws" more than they see the "beauty" in themselves? As human beings, all of us have at least *one* flaw in our lives. What flaws do you currently have in your life? Write down your personal flaws. Once you have written down your flaws, start asking yourself questions like, "How can I remove the flaws out of my life?" and "What areas do I need to improve in my life?" In order to start working on altering your flaws, you first need to identify them. Asking yourself questions will begin the process of discovering your flaws.

In his book, *Giant Steps: Small Changes To Make A Big Difference,* the bestselling author and world-renowned speaker, Anthony Robbins, hit the nail right on top of the head when he said, "New answers come from new questions." The more questions you ask, the more you will learn. A curious mind is always thirsty for new solutions. As human beings, our minds are always curious about something; that is why our minds are constantly thinking about something every second. For instance, scientists' minds are continuously in *experimental* mode, as they ask themselves and their colleagues, "What if we try this with that?" Asking questions will make you better. Don't be afraid to ask yourself or others questions. Asking questions will lead you to the answers that will show you how to succeed. Moreover, asking questions will give you the opportunity to discover innovative solutions that will enable you to prevail in your endeavors.

The following is a metaphor that you could use for asking questions: Success is a ladder and each ring of the ladder is a question. If you try to skip over questions and don't ask them, you run the risk of missing the step and falling down. The gap is too wide when the question is unanswered. Step on each ring along the way–ask and answer each question–and soon you will find yourself closer to the top of the success ladder.

As a winner, ask yourself, "What do I want to achieve?" Once you have the answer to the previous question, ask yourself, "How can I achieve it?" As I've stated before, one reason many people don't succeed in their lives is because they never discover "what" they want to achieve in their lives. Asking yourself questions will wake up your mental creativity, which will allow you to produce new results in your life. Go ahead and be inquisitive. Questions lead to success. The moment you start asking yourself and others questions that will be the moment you will begin to win and achieve more in your life. The questions you ask will not only elevate *your* mind, they will also lift up the minds around you.

53

MAXIMIZE YOUR POTENTIAL

How are you currently applying your own potential?

There are over a million ways that you have the opportunity to succeed. One of the best ways to succeed is to maximize your own potential. If you had to take a survey on yourself, and you could only choose <u>one</u> answer, would you say that you're "maximizing" or "minimizing" your own potential? If you glanced around, you would begin to see the number of people who are *maximizing* and *minimizing* their potential.

Our *beliefs* are like a mental seesaw. It's our beliefs that attract limited and limitless opportunities–it depends on which one weighs the most in our minds. Have you ever placed *limits* on yourself? If so, how many limits have you placed on yourself? Have you mentally limited yourself by doubting yourself? Have you limited your expectations of what you can and cannot achieve? How many times have you told yourself, "I can't succeed?" The mental, emotional, and physical *limits* that you place on yourself will prohibit you from maximizing your own potential.

Why would you want to stay behind the starting line, when you have the opportunity and the potential to cross the achievement line? Why would you want to be average, when you can be extraordinary? Why would you want to take a *half* step, when you can take a *whole* step? In other words, why would you want to shortchange yourself, when you can have the best of everything?

Think of the previous questions as your mental alarm clock to wake you up. You may be thinking, what does Skip mean by *maximizing* my potential? When it comes to "maximizing" your potential, start striving for number one, instead of settling for number two, three, or four. Strive to be the best, instead of the worst. Strive for first place, instead of last place. When you give your best and go for the best, you will receive the best. Don't settle for average results; go for extraordinary results. You deserve more, so go for more in your life. You deserve the best, so go for the best things in life. You have unlimited potential, start *maximizing* it.

When your objective is to win, you must give your best effort. How can you give your best effort? Go all the way! Start maximizing your potential by committing yourself to achieve more in your life, on a daily basis. Start pushing and challenging yourself every single day. On your journey, a few people are going to try to stop you from succeeding, whatever you do, don't give them the satisfaction. Never let anything or anyone stop you from succeeding, even if that person is yourself. As a winner, you must do whatever it takes to prevail. You have an abundance of potential within you; don't waste your potential by not using it. Maximize your potential. You have your own uniqueness that is ready to be displayed for others to see. Once you begin to take advantage of your own potential you will enhance your opportunities to achieve more. The more action you take toward achieving your goals, the more you will discover the uniqueness of your own potentials and personal talents.

Every person has the ability to achieve something in his or her life. Every winner has a dream that he or she wants to achieve. As a winner, you have a dream, and you can achieve it. Since no one else can use your potential for you, why not go ahead and maximize your own potential? You have too much talent inside of you to let it go to waste.

As a winner, start taking advantage of your own potential. Regardless of what some people may have said about you or done to you in the past, today is your day to mentally, emotionally, and physically go beyond what others said you couldn't do. I'm not saying, "Go out and try to prove yourself to everybody." However, I am saying, "Put your potential where it belongs – in action." Set your mind and actions on what you want to achieve, and never take your mind and actions off of what you want to achieve, until you achieve it. Once you start maximizing your potential, golden opportunities will appear on your path that will lead you to the next level.

54

THE MAGIC OF CONFIDENCE

How secure are you with your own confidence?

Winners are confident people who believe in themselves. Winners' self-confidence levels are high because they have confidence in themselves and their abilities to succeed. Some people view winners as though they have a chip on their shoulders. However, that is not the case with all winners. Winners are not arrogant people; they are *confident* people.

Winners have inward confidence about themselves that continues to elevate them to new heights. Winners optimistically think and confidently believe they will succeed. If you were to put a wall in front of a winner, he or she would not just look at it as a "wall." They would view the wall as a challenge to test their self-confidence. This reminds me of the "obstacle course" in the Marine Corps. boot camp. In the midst of the *obstacle course*, we had various challenges placed in front of us like climbing ropes, climbing over walls, and crawling underneath barbwire, which all had to be accomplished within a certain amount of time. Although we faced a variety of obstacles, we overcame our challenges, which built up our self-confidence.

As Dr. Robert H. Schuller's book title states, *"Tough Times Never Last, But Tough People Do!"* As a winner, obstacles will appear on your journey, keep in mind that you are tougher than you think, so don't' let adversity defeat you. You may be presently going through a few obstacle courses in your life that are challenging you, keep your head up because you can overcome them. For instance, you might be living paycheck-to-paycheck. You may be one door away from being homeless. You could be a single parent. You may be facing numerous challenges in your life, but you can overcome them. Whatever you are currently going through in your life, there are thousands of people who overcame the same challenge. There are achievers who are ready to help you overcome your challenges. Each challenge will either strengthen or weaken your self-confidence. In *Feel The Fear And Do It Anyway,* Susan Jeffers declared the strength of overcoming challenges: "The world is filled with people who have been handed the "worst" life has to offer…and they have come out winners!"

Winners don't only push *themselves*; they also push their *self-confidence* to new levels. As a winner, begin playing toward your strengths, because it will be your strengths that will make your self-confidence stronger. When your self-confidence is strong, there is no such thing as defeat. Winners know there will be obstacles that will attempt to test their self-confidence. This is one reason why winners are constantly preparing themselves physically and mentally, because when obstacles occur, they will be ready to over their forthcoming challenges. As a winner, you must do the same. Start preparing yourself mentally, emotionally, and physically for your forthcoming challenges. Once you start preparing yourself, your self-confidence and success levels will grow to new heights.

Winners create and build their own success circles and positive environments. As a winner, you can build up your self-confidence by surrounding yourself with confident achievers. Also, start seeking and focusing on the positive things around you. Rather than looking for the negativity around you, start looking for the positivity around you. Once you look for the positivity around you, you will begin to view people, places, and things differently.

There is magic in having confidence in yourself. You don't have to be a magician to succeed, but you must have self-confidence to succeed. Self-confidence is one of the best-kept secrets for every success. Simply, because self-confidence is the "magic" behind success. It is the unseen element that motivates winners to succeed. The level of your self-confidence will start inviting the right people to "appear" into your life, while the negative people, places, and things will begin to "disappear" out of your life.

55

WHICH WAY DID YOU SAY AGAIN?

Your destination awaits you, which way will you go?

Real pleasure in life is not when you jump all over the map. Real pleasure in life is when you discover "where" you want to go, and arrive at your destination. Mediocre people jump all over the map because they haven't found a destination to aim toward, and arrive at in their lives.

Winners pick their destinations in life, and constantly aim toward what they want to achieve daily. The difference between a successful person and an unsuccessful person: Unsuccessful people *complain* about the mileage that it will take to reach their destination. Successful people *plan* and *prepare* themselves for the mileage that it will take to reach their destination. Are you complaining, or are you planning and preparing to reach your destination?

The renowned business philosopher and speaker, Jim Rohn once said, "We go the direction we face, and we face the direction we think." As a winner, you are the *driver* of your own life and victories. You are the *planner* of your life and success maps. You are the only person who knows where you want to go, and when you want to arrive at your destination. In life, you are your own red and green lights. You will either "stop" yourself from winning, or you will "drive" yourself to win. You are the decision-maker who will select the highways, roads, and paths that you will travel on to reach your ultimate destination. It doesn't matter how many people you ask, "Which way do I go?" It will be your own decisions, and actions that will lead you to your destination.

As human beings, we all encounter confusion at least once in our lives. One of the main reasons a lot of us travel through life confused is because we haven't found the right direction that we want to travel. For example, let's say you want to drive from New York to California. You have packed your car for the road trip.

You remembered everything you need for your trip. As you start your trip, you notice something is missing...you forgot the road map. Many of us are traveling every day through our lives without roadmaps or Global Positioning System (GPS) to navigate us to our next destination. Without a destination to aim toward, we encounter confusion, which causes us to wander through life without ever finding or arriving to our destinations. Do you know where you want to go in your life? Knowing *where* you want to arrive in your life, business, career, wealth, and relationships will place you on the right track to reach your destination. The starting point to reaching your destination is first identifying "what" you want to achieve, and "where" you want to go. Knowing these two principles will help you arrive faster.

Dr. Robert Schuller once stated, "What appears to be the end of the road may simply be a bend in the road." While on your journey, you may encounter a few bumps, setbacks, detours, dead ends and forks in the road, but don't let them discourage you from moving toward what you want to achieve. Remember, they are only *challenges*, and you can overcome your challenges.

Winners are planners. One secret to success: plan ahead. Stay *ahead* of the game, not behind the game. As a winner, you will need to plan and prepare yourself, so you can arrive at your destination successfully. Where would you like to travel? What would you like to achieve? Make a plan and work toward your plan every single day. Find something you want to achieve in your life, and stick to it like glue, until you achieve it.

As a winner, you have places to go, people to see, and goals to accomplish. Today is not the day to procrastinate. Today is the day to step outside of your comfort zone. Today is the day to take action toward achieving your dreams. Today is the day to challenge yourself to achieve something new. Today is the day to pull your life out of the driveway and drive it. Today is the day to elevate yourself to the next level. Today is the day to turn on the radio and enjoy the music to your ears. Today is the day to honk your own horn, so you can let others know you're coming through. Today is your day to arrive at your destination. Overall, today is your day to win!

56

THE WINNER'S MENTALITY

What thoughts are going through your mind as you strive to win?

As the real estate mogul, Donald Trump, once said, "I like thinking big. I always have. To me, it's very simple: if you're going to be thinking anyway, you might as well think big." There are various starting points in life. The starting line to winning begins in the nucleus of your mind. When your ultimate goal is to win, you first must mentally condition yourself to win. When was the last time you told yourself, "I am a winner?" The way you *mentally* view yourself will be the manner, in which you will *physically* present yourself.

Winners understand attitude is everything. This explains why winners present themselves in a positive manner, because they know having a positive mental attitude is essential. As W. W. Ziege once stated, "Nothing can stop the man with the right mental attitude from achieving his goal; nothing on earth can help the man with the wrong mental attitude." Having the right attitude matters. Likewise, winners have a "whatever it takes" mentality that is unshakable. Instead of being fearful and pessimistic, winners are *fearless and optimistic.*

If you told a winner, "It's impossible" or "You can't do it," he or she would quickly accept your statement, as an invitational challenge. When it comes to *challenges*, winners love to be challenged. Winners breathe and eat challenges for breakfast, lunch, and dinner. One reason most winners welcome challenges is because they are always looking for new challenges. A challenge to a winner is like a new adventure. Winners enjoy challenges because they know each challenge will do more than *dare* them–it will test, expand, and improve them.

There are three core ways to win: Test, challenge, and improve oneself. If you don't *test* yourself, how will you distinguish what your strengths and weaknesses are? All of us have weak areas in our lives that need strengthening. If you don't *challenge* yourself, how will you discover what you can accomplish in your life? You can accomplish more once you start maximizing your potential. If you don't *improve* yourself, how will you elevate yourself to the penthouse level of success? Remember, there is always a next level.

As a winner, you will face challenges. When you encounter challenges, what will you do? Will you do *whatever it takes* to conquer your challenges? Or will you play hide-n-go-seek, and hide behind your fears and excuses? Don't run from your challenges and fears; stand up to your challenges and fears. Some challenges will be strategically placed into your life to make you overcome your fears. This is why it's vital that you adopt the "Whatever it takes" attitude. As a winner, you must be willing to do whatever it takes to conquer your fears and adversities.

Your mind is its own unique treasure. Every decision you make starts inside of your own mind. You are the only person who knows exactly what you want to achieve in life. You can tell others what you want to achieve, but you always have the option to change your mind along the way. There is nothing wrong with changing your mind because you are the ultimate decision-maker of your life. At the end of the day, it will be your own decisions that will produce your actions, results, and achievements.

As a winner, it's never too late to think bigger. From the moment you wake, until the moment you go to sleep, you control the binoculars to the way you view life. You are the overseer of the direction in which your life and success sails. As the owner of your own mind, you can either think small or think big. The height of your thoughts will produce the height of your actions, results, and triumphs. When you think like a winner, you will become a winner. Start thinking and acting like a winner, because you are a winner!

57

GET STARTED

Did you forget to start the process?

The road to success doesn't start at the beginning of a "physical" road. The road to success begins once you physically take the first step toward what you want to achieve. Did you know "starting" is one of the hardest steps to every success? Many people know exactly what they want to achieve in their lives, but they never take the first step to "start" the process to achieve it.

A few days ago, I had an interesting conversation with a gentleman named Jack. During our conversation, Jack complimented me on the success of my book *Think Progress*. Jack told me that he would like to write a book one day. As I listened to him, I inquired, "What are you currently doing to write your forthcoming book?" Jack replied, "Currently nothing because I don't have the time to write my book. Once I start something, I like to keep going until the end." I liked Jack's positive attitude, however, I was a little questionable on his time management, so I extended his mental vision by asking him more questions.

The first question I asked Jack was, "Do you really want to write a book?"

He said, "Yes, but I don't have the time to write it."

Then I stated, "You may think you don't have the time to write, but you always have a little time for the things that you want to achieve, even if you only have a few seconds, minutes, or a few hours to put toward it."

Jack replied, "Once I start something, I like to go straight through it without distractions." I understood what he meant, but I wanted him to look at what he wanted to achieve from a different perspective.

"Jack," I said, "I understand you don't want distractions, but right now it sounds as though you're currently your own distraction."

In a dumbfounded manner, Jack replied, "What do you mean?"

I stated, "I noticed you keep saying that you don't have the time. If you typed just one page a day, in 365 days, you would have a 365-page book."

After thinking about what I had just said, Jack said, "I never thought about that."

I said to Jack, "If you really wanted to, you could type one to three pages a day. One reason you haven't started writing your book is because you're trying to complete it all at one time. Since you can't write and complete your book all at once, you don't want to start."

Surprised from my observation, Jack replied, "You're right."

In conclusion, I told Jack, "Start writing your book in increments. If you don't have a lot of time, write one to three pages every day, and before you know it your book will be complete." Don't let the *starting* process stop you from achieving your dreams. One reason most people don't "start" taking action toward their dreams is because they think that they have to achieve their dreams all at once, which is not true. Winners understand success is achieved in increments–not all at once. As we all know, Roman wasn't built in one day. If you have to *start* small, start there. If you have to get up early or stay up late to achieve your goals and dreams, start there. Once you start the process, the closer you will get to crossing the achievement line.

As a winner, your success doesn't *start* the moment someone tells you, "You've succeeded." Your success starts the moment you tell yourself, "I *will* succeed." You will win, once you *start* the process. You will excel, once you *start* aiming higher. You will achieve more, once you *start* believing in yourself more. Start taking *one to three* action steps toward your goals every day. The secret to winning is to *start* the momentum. Once you *start*, you will be amazed how fast you will achieve your goals and dreams.

58

SUCCESS IS BEYOND YOUR FEARS

What do you fear the most?

As Susan Jeffers' book title states, *"Feel The Fear And Do It Anyway."* To win, you must go beyond your own fears. Your success is on the other side of what you fear. As a winner, you must ignite your determination to go beyond what you fear. When you go beyond the things you fear, you will not only discover your success, you will also place yourself on the side of victory.

Every person fears something, but winners overcome their fears. Winners refuse to let fear intimidate them because they do whatever it takes to become fearless. When you believe in yourself, and you know exactly what you want to achieve–what is there to fear? Whatever you fear, you can overcome it. Determination overrides fear. During several surveys, many successful people were asked, "What do you think holds most people back from succeeding?" FEAR was at the top of every list. Most people *fear* public speaking. Many people *fear* failing. Some people *fear* success. While others *fear* the unknown. Which one do you fear: failing, success, or the unknown? Fear will keep you from succeeding in your own life. Fear will try to trick you into believing that you won't succeed. Your fears will cause you to worry and experience anxiety.

As a kid, what were some of your fears? Was one of your fears riding a bike for the first time? We all remember the "training wheels" days. While riding our bikes with the training wheels on, no one could tell us anything, because the training wheels had our back. Then came the day the training wheels were removed off of our bikes. Yes, we were happy to have a bike, but we were nervous to get *on* the bike, because the training wheels were gone. Although you were nervous without the training wheels, you still hopped on your bike and rode it.

What is another one of your fears? What about riding the roller coaster for the first time? Do you remember how afraid you were to sit in the seat? The safety rail came down across your lap. Then the roller coaster slowly started moving forward. The next thing you knew, the roller coaster had picked up speed. Then as it went down the first hill, you noticed your fellow riders began to hold up their hands, so you joined in and put up your hands too. Then came the sharp curves, and we can't forget the peak area–where the roller coaster slowly climbed to its highest point–and your heart started to beat faster, due to the adrenaline rush and the anticipation of what was coming up next, beyond the hill. Do you remember how fast your heart was beating? When you encounter fear it can make your heart beat fast. Fear is like the first time you rode a bike, and the first time you rode a roller coaster. Though you were afraid, the rush of fear was good and you liked it. It was the adrenaline rush of the fear that made your heart race, and what motivated you to want to ride again.

To win in life, you must be willing to unleash yourself to do whatever it takes to win. When it comes to fear, you have <u>three</u> choices: You can either let your fears defeat you, put your fears underneath your feet and step on them, or you can use your fears as your motivator. As I like to say, "I step on top of my fears. I don't let my fears step on top of me." Also, I use my fears to motivate me. Most winners use fear to their advantage. Rather than backing down to challenges, winners use their fear as strength to overcome their challenges.

As a winner, always remember, your success is *beyond* your fears. Fear is the wall that is standing between you achieving or not achieving your dreams and goals. You can overcome fear by accepting that your fear exists, and using your fear as strength to climb over the "fear" wall. Fear is the gatekeeper that holds most people back from succeeding. Don't let your fear hold you back. Use your fear to motivate you to aim higher. Become fearless! Keep in mind fear is an "internal bully" that you can internally overcome and defeat. The next time you encounter fear: Feel the fear and do it anyway.

59

WHAT'S INSIDE OF YOU?

How often do you think about what is really inside of you?

Whenever we think about what is "inside" of us, we quickly think about the blood, organs, veins, and the heart. There is a lot more *inside* of you than you think. What you have *inside* of you is infinite.

Yes, we have blood pumping inside of us. Yes, we have organs and veins inside of us. Yes, we have our own brains and hearts inside of us. As a winner, you have to have *heart* to win. Most winners call this "The Heart of a Champion." Are you using your own brain and heart to thrive or to survive? You have a heart, but how are you using it? Are you wholeheartedly committing your mind, determination, action, and persistence to what you want to achieve? Are you reading books and asking people questions that will enhance your mind with innovative knowledge? Are you exercising your mind and body to be the best person that you can be?

Yes, you do have a heart, but what are you doing to keep your heart and life pumping, so you can win in life? Are you sitting down with your feet kicked up eating unhealthy foods, or are you exercising, and eating healthy foods? It's very easy to blame others, who are on the outside of us, for our unwanted results. As winners, we must take the initiative to become responsible for ourselves. If you're constantly staying inside of the house eating with your feet kicked up and looking at TV, how do you expect to win? You can blame others, but you also must blame *yourself* for your own actions and results.

The most difficult task about winning is getting people to use what is already inside of them. Most people know the qualities that they have inside of them, but many of them don't know how to use their internal strengths. There are so many attributes inside of us that we get confused by trying to decide which ones to use.

Muhammad Ali, the boxing legend, was renowned for displaying his personal greatness through his boxing skills, and for verbally calling himself "The greatest of all time." There is greatness within you. It's what's *inside* of you that will differentiate you from others. Winners recognize, value, and utilize what they have inside of them. You may be thinking, "What do I have *inside* of me?" You have an abundance of outstanding qualities inside of you that are ready to be displayed. The following are just a few distinctive characteristics that you have inside of you:

- Creativity
- Confidence
- Determination
- Value
- Ideas
- Courage
- Passion
- Integrity
- Forgiveness
- Competence
- Excellence
- Commitment

In his book *"Little Voice" Mastery*, Blair Singer declared, "Inside you, there's a champion and a loser. There's an angel and a devil. There's a hero and a villain. The question is, which one is going to win today?" You are a winner, which means there is a "winner" inside of you.

As a winner, you possess an endless list of extraordinary attributes. Once you start utilizing your internal strengths, your possibilities will be endless. When you turn on your internal engine, and combine your mind, actions, and persistence together, you will begin maximizing your unique qualities. As a winner, you know what is inside of you, start using it. When you apply what is inside of you, you will begin to display your own greatness.

60

YOUR OWN BEST FRIEND

What are you doing to become your own best friend?

In his compelling book, *Think Like A Winner*, Dr. Walter Doyle Staples observed, "You are your own worst enemy when you continually tell yourself you cannot succeed. You must learn to become your own best friend by making your internal success mechanism work to your advantage." When you look at yourself in the mirror, how do you see yourself? Do you see yourself as your own "best friend" or as your own "worst enemy?"

A few people have asked me, "Why do I seem so comfortable everywhere I go?" Here is my secret: I have learned how to become my own best friend. For some people, this is a difficult task. However, it's really not that hard to become your own best friend. Becoming your own best friend means spending quality time with yourself. I know a few people who refuse to go to the movie theater, or to a restaurant by themselves. You may be thinking, "How is that possible?" Because they are afraid to be alone. They would rather seek *outside* friends to entertain them, instead of spending quality time with themselves, so they can become their own best friend.

Many people are uncomfortable with themselves, because they haven't become their own best friend. Have you ever noticed how some people go overboard looking for friends? They hang out at the clubs, bars, on the street, and casinos looking for friends. They say and do things that they really don't want to do or say, but they do it anyway just to seek friendship. In other words, they try to fit into someone else's circle. "If I could only get into that circle of friends" the person desperately thinks and says to oneself, assuming the particular group of people will make him or her happier as a person. As a winner, you don't have to fit into someone else's circle to be happy. You can create your own circle of winners and be happy.

Self-improvement starts within oneself. Millions of people encounter doubt, desperation, and depression because they look "outside" of themselves more than they look "inside" of themselves. Sure, we seek "outside" ourselves for friendship, but we forget to look "inside" ourselves for friendship. It's not the people *outside* of you that will make you happy. It will be the *inner friendship with yourself* that will make you happy. You will discover happiness when you have an internal rapport with yourself. You can look for external friends for comfort, but you will need to become your own *internal* best friend to become comfortable with yourself and your surroundings. What if all of your friends were unavailable, what would you do? Would you keep calling and texting them until someone responds? Would you flip through all of the TV channels to see what's on? Or would you spend quality time with your internal best friend?

You might have a large number of friends; nonetheless, you need to become your own best friend. When you become your own best friend, you will discover the treasure to your own happiness. One reason countless people are unhappy in their lives is because they haven't found their own personal happiness. It's interesting how we can look "outside" of ourselves, and see other people who are happy in their lives, but we refuse to look "inside" of ourselves to seek our own personal happiness. Happiness is an inside job. The best place to find your own happiness is to start *within* yourself. The more quality time you spend with yourself during your self-appointments, the more you will discover what makes you happy.

Winners overlook the negativity of what people think or say about them, because they have internally accepted themselves as their own best friend. As a winner, become your own best friend. External "friends" (people, alcohol, drugs) will give you temporary comfort. When you become your own *internal* best friend, you will be comfortable wherever you go. When you are with your friends, you usually feel comfortable around them. The same scenario happens once you *become your own best friend*, you will begin to feel comfortable with yourself.

61

LISTEN. LISTEN. LISTEN.

What did you hear today that could change your life?

John C. Maxwell's book title, *Everyone Communicates, Few Connect,* hits the nail on the head. Every person wants to talk and be heard, but only a few people open their ears and minds to listen. The people who listen usually achieve more. Winners are *listeners.* When others talk, winners listen. As a winner, keep in mind that listening is an important communication skill.

Though all of us have the opportunity to communicate, there are some people who talk more than they listen. I'm sure we all know a few talkative people. *Listening* is a valuable quality that is often overlooked. When it comes to listening, we "hear" what is being said, but are we truly "listening" to what is being said? We talk about what we are going to do, what we would like to do, and about what we have already done. After all the *talking,* what else is left? It's called *listening.* Simply taking a moment to listen could reward you in various ways.

While having a conversation with someone are you really *listening* to the person, or are you *thinking ahead* to what you're going to say next in the conversation? Research studies show that we can think faster than we can talk. However, sometimes we need to slow down our thinking to grasp what is being said to us. When you take the time to listen, you will show others how much you value, respect and appreciate them. Also, you will learn how to win faster when you listen.

If we constantly go around talking, talking, and talking–when would we ever learn? We learn when we *listen.* When you minimize your talking and start maximizing your listening, you will enhance your knowledge, and gain more leverage to excel in your life. Winning is not about how much you talk. Winning is about how much you listen, learn, and apply. The more you listen, learn, and implement what you have learned–the more you will soar, thrive, and win. Successful companies *listen* to their customers. Likewise, winners succeed because they seek innovative resources, and listen for the clues and strategies that will advance them to the next level.

"When you look and listen, you will always get your answers."

Winners know success leaves clues. This is one reason why winners keep their eyes and ears open, because they are always looking and listening for new techniques to succeed. Listening is a priceless quality that we all have once we decide to use it. The benefit to listening is that you will continuously learn something new. When you listen, you will discover creative ways to improve yourself, wealth, and success. Listening and observing others is one way I learned how to succeed. Instead of talking, I listened, watched, and modeled the successful people. When you look and listen, you will always get your answers. The answers that you're seeking are only a listening experience away. *Listen* as though your life depended on it. *Listen* for the clues and gems that will help you win. *Listen* as if someone is giving you the winning numbers for you to win the $100 million lottery jackpot.

There are some people that talk so much that they forget to listen. Rajesh Setty, the author of *Beyond Code: Learn to Distinguish Yourself in 9 Simple Steps!* declared, "When you listen, you will gain invaluable insights into a person's values, beliefs, and priorities." As a winner, the next time you're having a conversation with someone, let the other person talk more than you. Sometimes it's good to take the backseat in the conversation and let someone else drive it. I stated to one of my long-winded friends, "You don't have to try to dominate the conversation. It's okay to *share* the conversation." When you share the conversation with others, it will allow both of you to talk, listen, and learn something. The more you *listen*, the more you will learn. The more you *learn* how to listen, the more leverage you will have to become your own unstoppable force.

62

WINNERS STAND UP

If you could stand up, would you stand up?

Will the real "winner" please stand up? This question should have empowered you to jump up. YOU ARE A WINNER! There is a *winner* inside all of us. The moment you wake up in the morning, the first thought that should go through your mind is "I am a winner!" Winners think like winners, even while they are sleeping.

On numerous occasions, I have been asked, "Why do people think and call themselves *losers*?" Many people think and call themselves losers because someone or a few people once upon a time called them a "loser." Although the person could have had this uttered to them years ago, the little voices that *used to* call them a loser, continues to linger inside of their heads. One of my clients told me about the little voices that he hears inside of his head. He frequently hears several voices saying the following:

- "You're a loser."
- "You'll never amount to nothing."
- "You're just like your father/mother."
- "Your brother is smarter than you."

Although this scenario happened to my client, I'm sure that you have a few words that you could add to the previous list. Blair Singer, the author of *"Little Voice" Mastery,* affirmed, "Your 'little voices' are really the sum of all the experiences and advice you have had in your life." As winners, we must understand that the words people use and throw at us are just that...they are only "words." We cannot *physically wear the words* that people verbally call us. Can you imagine everyone walking around wearing all of the words that they were labeled since they were a kid? It sounds ridiculous, because it is ridiculous. Why would you want to continue wearing other people's daunting words all over your mind and body for the rest of your life?

The author, federal grant researcher and informational personality, Matthew Lesko is known for wearing colorful eye-catching suits with *questions marks* all over them. Mark is known as "the question mark guy." The reason I mentioned Mark Lesko is because he wears the question marks on the "outside," while countless people are wearing questions "inside" of their minds, as they continue to ask themselves, "*Why* is this happening to me?" The same way fashion changes every season, you can change your mental wardrobe every day. Throw away the "old" words that people once said about you. Choose "new" words that will empower you daily. Look into your own mental closet, and select what you will mentally and physically wear today.

You can tell a winner when you see one, because he or she will always stand out in the crowd. Some of us have been sitting down so long in our lives that we have forgotten that we have the ability to stand up. Winners are known for standing up for what they believe in. What do you believe in? Do you believe in yourself? If so, stand up for yourself. If you believe in a particular person, team, business, charity or law, stand up for it. Whatever you believe in, stand up for it. One reason the world seems to remain the same is because not enough people are willing to stand up for what they believe in. Instead of standing up for what they believe in, they choose to sit down, lie down, or accept whatever life presents to them. In order to win anything, you must be willing to stand up for what you believe in.

As a winner, stand up and step up for what you believe in. If you don't stand up, you will either get stepped on or stepped over. When you stand up for what you believe in, you will not be denied. Most importantly, when you *stand up*, you will *stand out* as a winner!

63

THE CERTIFIED WINNER

Are you ready and determined to do whatever it takes to win?

In life, there will always be challenges. Challenges are a part of life. Many people will embrace their challenges. A few people will run away from their challenges. Winners stand up and overcome their challenges. Some of us will encounter more challenges than others, because we place ourselves in challenging environments.

Winners welcome challenges, due to the excitement that each challenge brings them. Mike Krzyzewski, head coach of the Duke University men's basketball team and author of *Beyond Basketball*, stated, "There are always new and wonderful challenges out there, and part of maintaining success is knowing when you need to accept them." Winners love to be challenged. Winners believe if they are not being challenged, they are wasting their time, energy, and life away. To excel in life, you must be willing to challenge yourself every day. Start asking yourself, "How can I *challenge* myself today?" This question alone will get your mind and body moving. When you look for more ways to challenge yourself, you will discover innovative ways to elevate yourself to new levels. It's the winners who continue to challenge themselves and keep elevating to new heights. Winners stand out from the average crowd because they are constantly pushing themselves above and beyond the status quo. Instead of being complacent with what they have already achieved, winners continuously search for productive ways to achieve more.

How do most winners achieve more? They perpetually challenge themselves to go beyond their previous accomplishments. While some people look for ways to go the extra *inch*, winners seek ways to go the extra *mile*. For example, when the NBA Hall of Famer, Michael Jordan, played basketball he constantly pushed himself to the next level. His intensive work ethic was astonishing. Although he won six championships rings, he continued to set higher standards for himself to accomplish more. Today, some NBA and college players model themselves after Michael Jordan's standards. Why? Because Michael Jordan is a *certified winner*.

As a winner, are you striving to push yourself to new heights or are you satisfied with the level that you're currently at? Winners are never satisfied. Being "average" is never on the radar for winners. Being "the best" is always the target for winners. As a winner, what will you do today to win? Will you give your best performance? Will you go the extra mile? Will you go beyond what you have already accomplished? These are the questions that push and challenge winners every single day. Winners know they are the only individuals who can answer the previous questions.

Ask yourself, "What can I do today to go beyond what I have already accomplished?" Once you surpass what you have already accomplished, you will not only achieve more, you will stand out from the average, as a certified winner. One effective way to become a certified winner is by continuously improving yourself every day. The more you improve yourself, the better you will get, and the more you will win. Underachievers *settle* for what they have already accomplished. Do you want to be an underachiever or the best? The choice is yours. When it comes to being average or being the best, the latter will give you the opportunity to enjoy the best rewards. If you know that you have the ability to be the best, why would you want to settle for being average? Start setting higher standards that will push you to give your best performance daily.

As a winner, what are you doing to challenge yourself every day? Every person encounters challenges in his or her life. If you're currently being challenged in your life, what are you doing to overcome your challenges? Your challenges are here right now; what are you going to do about them *right now*? Will you stand up and conquer your challenges or will you settle for being average? One way to rise above your challenges is to go face-to-face with them. At the end of each day, ask yourself, "Did I *challenge* myself today?"

64

LIVE FOR THE BEST

If you could have the best, what would you do to receive the best?

Every winner's goal is to be the best. Every winner wants to have the best things that life has to offer. Every winner tells himself or herself, "I am the best!" As a winner, what are you doing every day to obtain "the best" things in life?

How many winners do you know who are proud that they came in *last* place? How many winners have you heard say, "I am going to strive to have the *worst* day of my life today?" How many winners have you seen that enjoys *losing*? The answers to the previous questions: ZERO! Why? Because winners refuse to lose. Winners strive to make every day their *best* day. Winners are always striving for *first* place. Every day we go through life either taking *half* or *whole* steps. Winners take the steps that will lead them to victory. Why would you want to take half steps, when it's only going to give you the short end of the stick? Why not take whole steps, so you can have the *whole* stick?

The following phrase is one that I use to challenge myself every single day: "If it's not *the best*, I don't want it." This explains why I present myself in a particular manner. Instead of half-stepping, I like to take *whole* steps by going all out. Instead of minimizing my life, I am constantly looking for more ways to improve and maximize my life.

In my early years, when I was growing up in Decatur, Georgia, my family didn't have much money. I was the only child, but I wasn't spoiled. There were plenty of times when I didn't receive what I asked for mainly because we couldn't afford it. One defining moment in my life was when I learned that there were more opportunities in the world. Growing up, I was limited and didn't see much of the world, because my family didn't travel outside of Georgia, so I only saw and heard about the world through looking at magazines, watching TV, and hearing stories that people told me. As an adult, I have traveled to various locations, such as New York (where I live), California, Miami, Chicago, New Orleans, Jamaica, and more fun-filled places.

What I have seen and learned on my journey has opened my mind to want to see and achieve more in my life. One valuable lesson I learned in my life: When you open your mind to new possibilities, new opportunities will present themselves to you. Every dream and every victory starts in the mind. This is one of the main reasons why I wrote this book: When you *think big*, you will *win big!*

"The best is always available to the person who wants the best."

Aim for the best things that life has to offer. The best is always available to the person who wants the best. Winners are not afraid to view life from their own perspective, instead of from society's point of view. Winners see themselves as the best! This occurs mainly because every winner strives to be *the best*. As a winner, never be afraid to say, "If it's not *the best*, I don't want it." When you *aim* for the best, you will eventually hit your target. When you *want* the best, you will do whatever it takes to make it happen. When you *give* your best, your results will display your performance.

In his book, *Think Like A Champion*, Donald Trump stated, "Don't ever think you've done it all already or that you've done your best. That's just a shortcut to undermining your own potential. Unless you've already kicked the bucket, there's still a lot more you can do." As a winner, never settle for less than your best. Set goals that will give you the opportunity to enjoy the best things in life. You are a winner, so aim to win. From this day forward, literally start telling yourself, "I am the best!" Most importantly, always give your best effort to be the best person that you can be.

65

IT'S GAME TIME

What level are you playing on today?

Winners enjoy playing the game because they know that's where the fun begins. Every day we mentally, emotionally, physically, and voluntarily choose the levels that we play on. Many years ago, I played various sports like baseball and basketball. But my favorite sport was football. When I played football, it was as though I was literally in another world, which most people call "being in the zone."

Before each game, I visualized myself succeeding, which usually set the tone for my forthcoming results. When it was time for me to physically go on the field, I literally told myself, "It's game time!" Today, I still use those same three words. Every time I step in front of an audience, it feels as though I'm stepping onto the football field, because my mind is extremely focused, and my enthusiasm is at peak level. When I played football, I gave my best. When I step in front of an audience, I give my best.

Today, I use my passion to help more and more people succeed, simply by telling myself, "It's game time!" In order for this technique to be effective, your passion must become your obsession. First, you will need to find something that you are passionate about. What are you passionate about? It could be something from your past, present, or future. Once you become passionate about something, it will internally ignite you to take physical action toward it. For example, there are professional athletes, musicians, singers, and actors who are full-time entertainers, because they have found something they are *passionate* about.

Winners are action and result-oriented. There may be times when you think, how did a particular person succeed? It's simple. The person took action. Lack of action will keep you as a spectator, while the action-oriented people continue to play and enjoy themselves on the field. There are millions of people who are full-time success stories. These are the achievers that we read and hear about via television, the media, Internet, and books. It's interesting how we can witness the success of others, yet some of us quickly tell ourselves, "I can't succeed." You *can* succeed. In order for you to succeed, you will need to start taking action steps that will lead you to succeed. Strive to become an *overachiever*, instead of an underachiever. When you strive to become an overachiever, you will continuously surpass the underachievers who are only striving to become average. The more you give your best performance, the more others will begin to admire and witness your success.

"Commit yourself to achieving your dreams, ideas, and goals."

As Jim Rohn once said, "If you work on your *job*, you can make a living. If you work on *yourself*, you can make a fortune." As a winner, start working full-time on improving yourself. Work on who you are as a person, a friend, a teammate, an entrepreneur, and as a provider for your family. Work on fixing, eliminating, and improving your personal flaws. Work on creating a better *you*. When you work on improving yourself, not only will you begin to produce effective results, you will enhance the quality in your finances, job, relationships, and life. Go full-time toward what you want to achieve. Go all out by giving all you've got to give. Commit yourself to achieving your dreams, ideas, and goals. Once you commit yourself to what you want to achieve, you will become a full-time achiever, which means there is no time to waste on unnecessary things.

As a winner, you must seek and find your passion. Once you discover your passion, tell yourself, "It's game time!" The game has started. Put on your game face and get in the game. Remember the winners' motto: "Work Hard. Play Hard." Most importantly, give your best effort to win the game.

66

LET THE GAMES BEGIN

What actions are you taking to make today victorious?

If you could make life a game, would you set rules to the game? If so, what rules would you set? If you could make life a game, would you play to win, or would you be a spectator in the stands? If you could make life a game, how much effort would you put forth to become the best person who ever played the game?

When you want to win and be the best–you will need to elevate your game. Success doesn't start on the sidelines. Success starts when you get on the field and play the game. There is a gigantic difference between "wishing" about what you want to achieve, versus "taking action" toward what you want to achieve. *Wishing* will paint a transient picture in your mind about what you want to physically achieve. When you *take action* toward your wishes, you will physically achieve what you wished for.

Winners don't win in life because they play somebody else's game and by someone else's rules. How successful do you think you will be if you're always playing someone else's game and by others' rules? Over and over again, I hear people say, "I want to start my own company." It sounds good to hear, but countless people never follow through on starting their own companies. For instance, I recall talking with one of my friends named Frank about starting his own company. In the midst of our conversation, Frank stated, "I want to start my own company."

I replied, "That's great Frank. When are you going to open the doors to your company?"

He was thrown by the question. Then I said, "If you want to start your own company, you will need to delete the habit of procrastinating." One thing I've noticed about Frank is that he's a procrastinator. Instead of following through on completing tasks, he procrastinates.

In conclusion, I stated, "Frank, when you really want to start your own company, you will need to get in the habit of mentally and physically following through on what you want to achieve." Talk is cheap. Action is priceless. When you turn your talking into action, you will see your results by what you accomplish.

> *"Winners understand that following through*
> *is a requirement for victory."*

Winners continuously create their own game plans and maximize their potential daily. Every day winners seek, discover, and develop new ways to enhance themselves, their skills, and their results. The lack of following through is one reason people don't succeed. Winners understand that following through is a requirement for victory. Moreover, winners know they must follow through for their game plan to successfully work.

How many game plans are you following? Are you following your boss' game plan? Are you following your parent's game plan? Are you following everyone else's game? Or are you following your *own* game plan? If you are following others' game plan, what are you doing to create your *own* game plan? Jim Rohn was correct when he said, "If you don't design your own life plan, chances are you'll fall into someone else's plan. And guess what they have planned for you? Not much."

There is a requirement for success. The requirement entails creating your own game plan, and physically following through until you succeed. As a winner, you must follow through until you achieve your ideas, goals, and dreams. Make life a game. Get in the game and have fun. Set limitless rules for yourself that will enable you to win daily. The game has begun. What actions are you going to take to become the best person who has ever played the game?

67

DRIVEN TO WIN

*Do you need an internal chauffeur to drive you
to your destination?*

Every person and every winner is *driven* by something. Winners
succeed because they are mentally, emotionally, and physically
driven. Some winners are *driven* by their life purpose. Some
winners are money-*driven*. Some winners are *driven* to be the best
person that he or she can be. Some winners are *driven* to prove
others wrong. Some winners are ego-*driven*. What is *driving* you?

Inside every winner is an internal driving force to win. For
example, Mark Cuban, the NBA owner of the Dallas Mavericks, is
driven by competition. Just the thought of competing is his
personal driving force. Nora Roberts, J.K. Rowling, Stephen King,
and James Patterson are all renowned bestselling authors. Has the
thought ever occurred to you as to what drives these extraordinary
authors? Though their creative minds are filled with exceptional
breathtaking stories, they are all driven to create a product that
readers will embrace. As winners, they are constantly challenging
themselves internally and externally to outperform what they have
already achieved. Instead of settling and being complacent about
the success of their previous bestseller books, they keep
challenging themselves to write more bestselling books. In their
minds, they aren't competing against others–they are competing
against *themselves*, as they continually write more books to surpass
their previous accomplishments.

The college football Hall of Fame coach, Lou Holtz, once said,
"If what you did yesterday seems big, you haven't done anything
today." Winners know whatever they achieved yesterday, they can
outdo it today. Every day winners persistently challenge and drive
themselves to give their best performance. They know it will be
their best performance that will produce their best results.
Likewise, winners know the more they accelerate themselves to

give their best performance, the more they will improve themselves, so they can be the best.

Winners are the most determined people in the world. We are all internally awakened and driven by something. The moment we discover what drives us–we become driven. What drives you? What revs your inner engine? What gets you super excited? What are you so enthusiastic about that it makes you jump out of bed in the morning? What are you passionate about? Your passion and determination will continuously drive you to achieve more.

It's been said, "Time is too valuable to *waste*." From my point of view, "Time is too valuable to *wait*." Dr. David J. Schwartz, author of *The Magic of Thinking Big*, wrote, "People that get things done in this world don't wait for the spirit to move them; they move the spirit." Sitting around *waiting* for success to come to you gifted wrapped will <u>not</u> get you across the achievement line. Don't "wait" for someone else to come along to push you, because that person may never show up. As a winner, you must not only outperform your opponent–you must also outperform *yourself*. This is what separates the average from the best. The best will always do things that the average won't do. Your success is waiting for you–don't keep it waiting. In other words, whatever you want to achieve, it's waiting for you to achieve it. While others are waiting to cross their "finish" lines, keep driving yourself every day to cross your "achievement" lines.

As a winner, you must start and continuously "push" yourself across the achievement lines. Always remember, when you are competing against *yourself*–the game is never over. When it comes to winning, you don't have to be *an athlete* to win or to challenge yourself. You can *be yourself* and still challenge yourself to win. When you keep challenging and driving yourself daily, not only will you begin to achieve more, you will continue to elevate yourself to the next level. Keep striving to achieve more than you did yesterday, last week, or last year. The time has arrived for you to aim higher, and achieve more in your life...DRIVE YOURSELF TO WIN!

68

TREAT YOURSELF TO THE BEST

How will you treat yourself today?

The entrepreneur, television commentator, and NFL Hall of Famer, Mike Ditka, once stated, "Before you can win, you have to believe you are worthy." You are a unique person, which makes you a valuable person. Out of the billions of people throughout the world, there will never be another person exactly like *you*. As a winner, you need to know your self-worth. You must believe in yourself, recognize the value of yourself, and know the extent that you will go to win.

Treating oneself to *the best* is a reward within itself. Why? Because "treating" yourself is *rewarding* yourself. When it comes to winning, you will need to celebrate your victories along the way. Refusing to reward yourself on your journey will make you begin to question yourself, "Is it worth it?" When you treat yourself to "the best," it's definitely worth it.

Within the last 30 days, how many times did you treat yourself to something new? When was the last time you indulged yourself just because you wanted to reward yourself? As a winner, start giving yourself the permission to enjoy the best things in life. This is one of the main reasons why you work hard to become a winner, so you *can* have the best.

> *"The best things in life are not available only to the wealthy and lucky people. The best things in life are accessible to every person who wants the best things in life."*

As a winner, you can have the best of anything and everything you desire. Don't let the best things in life pass you by because you think you're not ready for them. It doesn't matter if you *do* or if you *don't* have a million dollars in your bank account, you can enjoy the best things in life. If you're making minimum wage working a 9-to-5 job, you can still enjoy the best things in life. The part most people overlook is that the best things in life are not available only to the wealthy and lucky people. The best things in life are accessible to every person who wants the best things in life. Stop telling yourself that you "can't" have the best. Start telling yourself that you "can" have the best. Once your mind believes, understands, and absorbs the thought that "You *can* have the best," you will begin to attract it into your life.

One exceptional way to reward yourself is by treating yourself with respect. As I have stated on more than a few occasions, "People will always *treat* you how YOU allow them to *treat* you." Likewise, people will *say* whatever YOU allow them to *say* to you. People will *waste* your time when YOU allow them to *waste* your time. Moreover, people will *depress* you if YOU allow them to *depress* you. As a winner, always treat yourself with *first-class respect* and others will follow your lead. When you continually treat yourself to the best, you will come across more ways to reward yourself with the best. One secret behind Donald Trump's success: He constantly seeks more ways to treat himself to the best things in life. Think about it. Why would you want to treat yourself to mediocre, when you can have the *best*? Don't accept average results or complacency, because it will derail you from winning and obtaining the best.

Winners celebrate their victories. How will you celebrate your victories? As a winner, keep in mind that treating yourself to the best doesn't always mean buying "material" things. Treating yourself also entails surrounding yourself with the best. Always associate yourself with the best people who *can* and *will* help you win. Attending networking events and charities will give you the opportunity to connect with the right people who can help you succeed. When you affiliate yourself with elite people, each person will give you valuable resources that will advance you to the next level. The more you learn and apply what you learn, the further you will continue to elevate yourself to the penthouse level of success. The more you treat yourself to the best, the more you will enjoy the best things in life.

69

THINK WIN-WIN

Are you thinking win, lose, or draw?

Every person has the capability to win something in his or her life. One secret to winning is to "think" about winning. If you never *think* about winning, how do you expect to win? Every winner views himself or herself, as a winner. When you think, believe, and act like a winner, you will produce effective and winning results.

Another secret to winning is to know "what" you want to win. Winners know what they want to win. They think about it, dream about it, and take endless action toward what they want to achieve every single day. If you don't know *what* you want to win, now is the time to start thinking about it. When you think about winning, also think about *what* you want to win. When you know *what* you want to win, you will make it a lot easier for yourself to win.

> *"One reason countless people don't win in life is because they don't know what they want to win or achieve in their lives."*

Some people think they don't succeed because they don't have the skills, knowledge, wealth, or connections. One reason countless people don't win in life is because they don't know what they want to win or achieve in their lives. When your mind doesn't know what you want it to achieve, your mind will sit still like a car in *idle* mode, because it doesn't have anywhere to go. In order to reach your destination, your mind needs to know what you want it to achieve, before it will lead you in the right direction to achieve it.

When you want to reach your destination and make power moves in your life, you will need to know your destination. Take your mind out of *park*, place it in *drive* mode, and start driving your mind to think bigger. Napoleon Hill, the author of *Think & Grow Rich*, stated, "Whatever the mind can conceive and believe it can achieve." When your mind knows what you want it to achieve, it's not hard to think bigger. The difficulty to thinking bigger occurs when your mind doesn't have a sense of direction. Your mind needs to be constantly reminded that it can think bigger. Surrounding yourself with other winners will enhance your mind to think bigger. When you encircle yourself with other winners and people who are smarter and more creative than you are, they will make you think bigger, due to their creativity, wisdom, and work ethics.

Winners think differently. This is one quality that makes them extraordinary. Winners will mentally push your mind to new heights. Associating yourself with other winners will give you the opportunity to springboard your ideas into success, as you bounce your ideas off of them. Winners will show you more than how to create your own big picture. They will show and tell you exclusively how they succeeded, which will enable you to succeed. The more you surround yourself with winners, the more they will teach you how to think like a winner. As I recently stated to one of my friends, "Sometimes it's not always about who you surround *yourself* with. It's always about who you surround your *mind* with." Who are you surrounding your mind with? When you surround your mind with the best, you will begin to learn from the best.

As a winner, make it a habit to think bigger daily. Every success and failure starts with how you condition your mind. Your mind controls the actions you take. The actions you take will produce your results. Once you condition your mind to think bigger, the things you once thought were impossible will begin to look more possible. Winners are optimistic thinkers. In their minds, they don't lose–they just think of other ways to achieve their ultimate goals. Start thinking positive more than negative. When you think positive, not only will you adopt the winner's mindset, you will also discover innovative ways to win and prosper in your endeavors.

70

LEARN AND MASTER

If you could learn anything in the world,
what would you learn how to master?

In chapter 6, I talked about "learning" the fundamentals. In this chapter, we are going to talk about how to "master" the fundamentals. Every winner learn the basics of what he or she wants to achieve, even if it includes taking a moment to read the manual to get a better understanding. Once you know what you want to achieve, make it your duty to learn how to *master* it.

One of the best ways to achieve your goals and dreams is to first learn the fundamentals of what you want to achieve. In his book, *Think Like A Winner*, Dr. Walter Doyle Staples wrote, "Whatever your chosen profession, find an expert in your particular field, explain what you are trying to accomplish, and ask how you should go about doing it. Experts are not only those above you in an organization. Many are your peers and your subordinates." Winners learn the fundamentals of what they want to achieve by asking questions, researching others, and by their own personal experiences, which are called "trial and error."

Once winners understand the fundamentals, they mentally and physically do their best to master what they want to achieve. When you learn the basics to what you want to accomplish, do your best to master it. Remember, winning is a process. Without going through the process, you will keep yourself from learning the essential techniques that will enable you to succeed.

As winners, we need to learn not only how to master what we want to *achieve*, we also need to learn how to master *ourselves*. When it comes to learning and mastering ourselves, we need to learn how to effectively master our personal actions, results, and thoughts. We need to master our communication and people skills. Moreover, we need to learn how to master our finances through saving and investing. Do you want to live your entire life financially challenged or would you like to become a *master* of your finances, so you can avoid being financially broke?

As the Chinese philosopher, Confucius, once declared, "I hear and I forget. I see and I remember. I do and I understand." The key to learning how to master your craft is to learn from the masters. This is one reason why most winners look for mentors. Mentors are masters in their craft. They will help you see new possibilities. They will guide you in new directions. They will give you the support and resources that you will need to succeed.

Masters are readers. Masters know how to *read books* and they know how to *read people*. In other words, masters know "when" and "if" you are serious about learning, so don't waste their time. One creative and effective way to learn from a master is by discovering which publications that he or she reads. When you *read* what winners read, you will *learn* what winners learn.

Do you have a mentor? If you don't have a mentor, start looking for mentors. You will be amazed what you will learn from them. Each mentor will do more than just show you how to win and achieve your goals. They will place you on the right paths that will lead you to the next level. Also, mentors will introduce you to other extraordinary achievers.

As a winner, look for "successful" mentors. Most winners seek mentors in their industry. Some winners have various mentors for different areas of their lives. For instance, you could have mentors for your business, finances, relationships and hobbies. Write down at least *three* successful people who have the resources and the skills that will help you achieve your goals. You may be thinking, "I don't know anyone who can help me succeed." We all know at least <u>one</u> person who can and will help us succeed. If you don't know someone who can help you, consider joining organizations in your local area. Look for mentors who will do more than introduce you to the fundamentals. Seek mentors who will teach you how to become a *master* in your personal and professional life.

71

THE WORLD OF WHY

Do you really know why you're doing what you're doing?

How often do you think, "*Why* am I doing what I'm doing?" As winners, we must invest in ourselves by utilizing our time wisely. Simply taking a moment to think about "what" you are doing, and "why" you are doing it can save you a lot of time. If you don't know *why* or *what* you are doing, not only will it place you in the circle of confusion, it will also deter you from winning.

As human beings, we are always doing something in our lives–reading, working, talking, watching TV, traveling, spending time with family and friends. However, some of us don't know "why" we are doing certain tasks. Though most of us are doing what we are supposed to be doing, we still need to take a second and ask ourselves, "*Why* am I doing this?" Do you know "why" you are currently doing what you're doing? Are you watching a particular TV show and hanging with the same group of friends, due to its become a habit? Are you working at your job because you love it or just for the paycheck? All winners know *why* they are doing what they're doing. For instance, there are winners who take action to challenge themselves, due to the satisfaction that it gives them. Next, are the winners who take action to take care of their family. Then, there are the winners who strive to achieve their dreams, because someone told them that they couldn't do it. If you notice, winners always attach a "why" to their actions.

Discovering and knowing your *why* will make you stronger. If you haven't achieved something in your life lately, it's probably because you haven't attached a *strong why* to your actions. When you understand *why* you're doing the things that you're doing, not only will your confidence level grow to new heights, but also you will discover your purpose. Having a *strong why* will make you stop procrastinating and doubting yourself. You may be currently doubting yourself, but once you start asking yourself, "*Why* am I doubting myself?" your *why* will activate your actions. For instance, if you're living paycheck-to-paycheck, and you're down to your last paycheck, due to losing your job, and your family are depending on you to provide for them–you will quickly discover your *strong why*, as you commence to do whatever it takes to take care of your family.

As a winner, it's vital that you know "why" and "what" you're doing because it will prevent you from going around and around in the circle of confusion. Once you discover your *why*, you will do whatever it takes to fulfill your *why*. For example, Olympic athletes are known for working diligently to make it to the Olympics. But, if you were to ask an Olympian, if his or her dream were to just make it to the Olympics, he or she would quickly say, "It's good to make it to the Olympics, but that's not the goal. The goal is to win the *gold* medal." If you notice, Olympians know *what* they want to achieve, and *why* they are working hard. As a winner, what are you willing to sacrifice to fulfill your *why*? Winners are never afraid to take risks and make sacrifices in their lives. This is what separates the winners from the losers. Underachievers *refuse to* take the risks and make sacrifices. Winners *constantly* take the risks and make sacrifices.

In his book, *Start With Why: How Great Leaders Inspire Everyone To Take Action*, Simon Sinek wrote, "When people know WHY you do WHAT you do, they are willing to give you credit for everything that could serve as proof of WHY. When they are unclear about your WHY, WHAT you do has no context." When you seek your "why," you will find your "why." Every winner seeks his or her *why* before, during, and after they succeed. In other words, you will constantly be in pursuit of *why* you're doing what you're doing. Most people think it's their "goals" that drives them. Actually, it's their "whys" that drives them. It will be your "whys" that will constantly push and drive you to do more in your life. As a winner, never be afraid of challenges. Take on your challenges and conquer them. At the end of the day, it will be your own "whys" that will perpetually challenge, push, and drive you to give your best every single day.

72

THE PURSUIT OF ACHIEVEMENT

*What are you in pursuit of: pleasure, sadness,
confusion, or prosperity?*

In the inspirational movie, *Pursuit of Happyness*, the actor Will
Smith starred as the real Christopher Gardner, which the movie
and the bestselling book were both based on. Christopher Gardner
was a struggling single father, who encountered numerous
obstacles and setbacks on his journey, such as falling behind on his
bills, getting divorced, sleeping in public bathrooms and homeless
shelters with his toddler son, Chris Jr. Although Mr. Gardner
experienced multitudes of challenges, he never gave up. In his
mind, he always knew that he could achieve more in his life, and
he was determined to make it happen, which he did. Christopher
Gardner went from rags-to-riches, as he went from a homeless
single dad to a successful stockbroker and entrepreneur.

Within his bestselling book, *Start Where You Are,* Chris Gardner
asserted, "You can take what you've got–no matter how minuscule
it may seem to be–and use your innate powers of ingenuity,
together with hard work and focus, and make something
meaningful of yourself and your life is fundamental to all
pursuits." At the beginning, most winners like to start their pursuit
by taking action toward their dreams, ideas, and goals. They view
this area as their starting line, because it will lead them toward
their "achievement" line. As human beings, we are all in pursuit of
something that will bring us gratification. Every day all of us are
seeking and pursuing something that will lead us toward one or a
few of the following:

- Success/Achievement
- Wealth/Debt-free
- Relationships
- Excellence

- Happiness
- Love
- Trust
- Understanding

As a winner, what are you in pursuit of? Are you in pursuit of happiness and achievement? Are you on a spiritual or financial pursuit? Are you in pursuit to enhance your relationships? Where is your pursuit leading you? As George Allen once stated, "One of the most difficult things everyone has to learn is that for your entire life, you must keep fighting and adjusting, if you hope to survive. No matter who you are or what your position, you must keep fighting for whatever it is you desire to achieve."

In order to achieve what you are in pursuit of, you must become a "go-getter." When you are in pursuit of achieving your goals and dreams, you will need to be a *go-getter*. The pursuit of achievement is for winners, not procrastinators. Procrastinators delay their actions toward what they want to achieve. Winners continuously take action toward what they want, until they achieve it. It's the winners who get up and achieve their dreams, while the procrastinators stay in bed and dream. It's the *go-getters* who are persistent to keep trying, until they win. It's the *go-getters* who refuse to fail. It's the *go-getters* who are willing to fight for what they believe in. It's the *go-getters*, who are determined to succeed. It's the *go-getters* who become the winners in life.

As a winner, you must become a *go-getter*. Whatever you want to achieve is waiting on you to pursue it. Will you take action toward what you want to achieve or will you procrastinate? Procrastination doesn't produce gratification, nor will it put food on the table. It will be your actions and persistence that will continuously take you across the achievement line. As the Chinese philosopher, Lao Tzu once said, "The journey of a thousand miles must begin with a single step." As a winner, you are standing at the starting line to what you want to achieve. Start your pursuit. Start where you are. Start with your ideas, dreams, and goals. Once you take the first step across the *starting* line, you will be one step closer to reaching your *achievement* line.

73

GET ACTIVE

How effective are your actions?

As one of my mentors stated to me, "I didn't succeed by sitting on my laurels and wishing upon a star. I became successful because I worked hard and put in the work to constantly improve myself." How many *lazy* winners do you know? Most winners are "active" in their lives.

Laziness doesn't exist in the mind of winners. Winners refuse to sit around wasting their time on the couch eating a ham sandwich, and looking at TV while thinking, "Oh yeah, um…I would like to be a winner." Winners are not couch potatoes. Sitting on the couch looking at TV is not the best way to utilize your energy. Sitting on the couch is an excuse for <u>not</u> using your energy. Winners know excuses are like cow manure. It smells bad and no one wants to be around it.

Every person would like to achieve something; however, winners get off their butts and make it happen. For instance, if I were to ask you, what took place on a particular TV show you would probably be able to tell me every detail–all the way down to the wardrobe the actors and actress wore on the show. Now let me flip the script. If I were to go up to one of the actors or actresses–on the same TV show that you just told me about–and ask them about *you*, what do you think they would say? Not only would they probably not know you, but also they would probably say, "I'm too busy maximizing my life." As a winner, you must do the same. Start maximizing your life by getting active daily. There are plenty of activities that you could partake in your community and throughout the world, other than just sitting at home, playing video games, surfing the Internet, and watching the world on TV.

One reason people get tired and lazy is because they get tired of doing the same old things in their lives. Boredom captures those who lack action. How do you overcome boredom? By getting active. One of the best ways to consume your energy is by getting active. Getting active means taking action. Without action, there is no success. In order for you to produce effective results to succeed, you will need to take action steps toward what you want to achieve. Simply taking one step forward toward your dreams, ideas, and goals every day will boost up your energy level, which will enable you to accomplish more in your life.

As a winner, what action steps are you presently taking to make "better" things happen in your life? There are millions of people who help companies achieve their goals and game plans. However, when it comes to creating their own goals and game plans, they never start the process. Do you have a game plan? If so, how effective is your game plan? If you don't have a game plan, why not? The core to winning is establishing a game plan that will enable you to win.

Every winner creates a game plan. Planning, action, persistence, and producing effective results are the essential keys to winning. When your objective is to win, you must have a game plan to win. When you create your own game plan, you create your own blueprint for success. Most underachievers don't succeed, simply because they lack a game plan. A game plan is like placing a certified approval on your success. Create your game plan. Study your game plan. Take action toward your game plan. Achieve your game plan.

Sean Stephenson declared, in his book *Get Off Your "But"* that, "If you can shift the body, you can shift the mind." Today is your day to shift your mind, body, and actions. GET ACTIVE! Get off the couch. It's time to throw away your excuses, and get off your butt. Do something different today. Instead of turning *on* the TV–turn *off* the TV. Go outside. Take a walk down the street or around the block. Go to the gym and workout. Go hiking. Go skydiving. No one is holding you back, except Y.O.U. You can go wherever you want to go. You can achieve whatever your heart desires. But, first and foremost, you're going to need to get off your laurels.

74

FORWARD AND UPWARD

*Which way are you traveling in life: forward, backwards,
sideways, or nowhere?*

When you visualize your success, do you see yourself looking
"backwards" at what you have already achieved, or do you
envision yourself looking "forward" to what you are about to
achieve? When your mission is to win, every day is the best
day to look *forward* and move *upward.*

As a winner, it will be your forward progress that will move
you upward. While underachievers are looking *backwards*
toward what they have already accomplished, winners are
looking *forward* to their next accomplishment. Rather than
dwell on their past, winners keep looking forward. If winners
make a mistake, they shake it off, and move on to the next
task. Start looking forward to what you will accomplish next.

We move forward and upward, once we learn how to move
forward and upward. If we never learn how to advance
ourselves to new levels, we will remain at the same level in
our lives. Staying at the *same* level is never on the to-do list of
winners. Winners are always seeking effective resources that
will elevate them to the next level. Winners know "learning
and applying" are two proven and powerful strategies to move
forward and upward. The concept behind "learning and
applying" is simple: *Apply* what you *learn.* When winners
learn something new, they immediately look for ways to *apply*
it. As a winner, you must do the same. How much have you
"learned" in your life? Out of everything that you have
learned, how much of it have you "applied" in your life? You
have *learned* an abundance of valuable lessons from reading
books, your parents, your mentors/teachers, and your personal
life experiences. Now, it's time for you to physically *apply*
what you have learned.

How many winners are you surrounding yourself with daily? When you want to be the best, surround yourself with the best. When you want the best results, surround yourself with the winners that will bring out your best. Winners encircle themselves with other winners, because they want to produce the *best* results. Networking is one of the prominent ways that most winners surround themselves with other winners.

Winners know *networking* will hoist them to the next level. When you want to expedite your success, multiply and diversify your networking. One benefit to networking is that you will get the opportunity to meet extraordinary achievers. The more achievers that you network with, the more opportunities you will receive to keep elevating yourself to new levels. Networking with the right people, in the right circles will enable you to produce winning results. When it comes to networking, you can network everywhere you go. You can network at social, corporate and charity events, at the supermarket, or you can create your own networking group.

Partnership is another effective way winners move forward and upward. As a winner, never be afraid to start a partnership with people who are smarter, wealthier, or more advanced than you. I call this "Partnership With Excellence." This is when winners join forces with other winners. Make it your duty to partner your talents, ideas, and knowledge with achievers who are in higher echelons than you. Why? Because the achievers in the higher echelons will help you excel to the top faster. To reach the top, you will need achievers who will help you reach the top. The same scenario applies for winning. To win, you will need winners who will help you win. It will be your partnerships with excellence that will continuously assist you across your achievement lines.

As a winner, keep looking at the bigger picture. Focus on what you will accomplish next. Start applying what you have learned. Begin networking with winners. While networking, seek innovative ways to partner your creative talents and ideas with excellence. You will reach the top, when you keep moving forward and upward.

75

THE VICTORY STARTS WITH YOUR BEST

*If you are not giving your best effort,
how do you expect to become the best?*

If you lived in a world where you knew there were no limitations, would you place *limits* on yourself? As human beings, we set our own individual limits to what we "can" and "cannot" achieve. As a winner, you must remove your limitations and continuously go beyond your limits by telling yourself, "I *can* succeed" and "I *will* succeed." When you go beyond your limitations, your success will be endless.

Some people perceive winners as though they are "super" human. At the beginning, and at the end of the day, winners are "human" just like you. For instance, winners wake up and put on their shoes and clothes, just like you. Winners have dreams, just like you. Winners are constantly pushing themselves, and their envelopes to the next level, just like you. Winners aren't afraid to do whatever it takes to win. Winners are extremely focused, determined, action and results-oriented individuals whose ultimate goal is to be the best person that he or she can be. As a winner, regardless of what time of day it is…your best always starts with *you*.

Every winner has to start somewhere. Why not start from where you are? As a winner, the starting line to your success starts with *you*. It will be your own ideas, determination, actions, and results that will continually place you inside the winner's circle. What will you do toward your dreams today? Will you get up or will you stay in bed today? Will you maximize or minimize your potential today? Will you strive toward what you *want to* achieve or will you settle for what you *have already* achieved? If you know that your "best" starts with *you*, when are *you* going to start giving your *best*?

If you're not striving to win every day, what are you striving toward daily?

"If you know that your "best" starts with you, when are you going to start giving your best?"

Every victory starts with a dream. Every winner has a dream that he or she is in pursuit of achieving. In his book, *Put Your Dream To The Test,* John C. Maxwell, the leadership expert and bestselling author, declared, "The real difference between a dream and wishful thinking is what you do day to day." What is more important to you: looking at your *favorite* TV show or living your *own* dreams? Think about it. The people on TV are already living their dreams. What are you doing to live your own dreams? Remember, your success doesn't start while you're sitting *on* the couch. Your success starts once you get *off* your laurels and take action.

In order to cross the achievement line, you first must cross your own *starting* line. As a winner, never interrupt someone whose goal is to succeed. Most importantly, never let someone interrupt you from succeeding, including yourself. In other words, *you* are the only person who can hold you back from achieving your own dreams, ideas, and goals. Don't let your excuses, your past, or the unknown hold you back from moving forward and upward.

As a winner, *you* are standing at the entrance to your own success mountain. Will you get on the greatest ride ever made or go home? You have the master keys to unlock your own success doors. Will you unlock your success doors or will you let them stay locked? Today is the *best* day to give your best. Today is the *best* day to create new habits. Today is the *best* day to discover your whys. Today is the *best* day to get off your butt and get active. Today is the *best* day to put on your shoes and chase your dreams. Today is the *best* day to start a partnership with excellence. Today is the *best* day to start creating your own masterpiece. As a winner, today is the *best* day for you to think and win big!

POSTSCRIPT

As an author, it's rewarding to receive feedback from the readers. If you have any comments that you would like to share, I would love to hear from you. While reading *Think & Win Big*, did a particular story, quote, or strategy inspire you? What life-changing lessons did you learn? How have you applied what you learned? How did *Think & Win Big* help you? Every day you have the opportunity to reach for new and higher levels–reach for the stars.

Your success matters to me. At Skip Williams Communications LLC, the ultimate goal is to help *you* succeed. This is the core reason why I continue to push myself and burn the midnight oil, even in the daytime, because I want to help you achieve your dreams and goals. Every day I work around the clock seeking, discovering, developing, and revealing the world's best strategies that will enhance and maximize the quality of your life, performance, results, and success.

For more information about products, services, and forthcoming events, or if you would like to inquire about my availability as a speaker for your next event, you can contact me via:

Skip Williams Communications LLC
P.O. Box 7071, New York, NY 10116

Phone: 646-580-8405
E-mail: skip@skipwilliamsonline.com
www.skipwilliamsonline.com

ABOUT THE AUTHOR

Skip J. Williams is an author, professional speaker, and entrepreneur. Mr. Williams is the founder and CEO of Skip Williams Communications LLC, a personal and professional development firm specializing in leadership, entrepreneurship, peak performance, and executive coaching. Skip is also known as "The Next Level Coach," due to his never-ending commitment to elevate his clients and audiences to the next level. His exceptional life-changing strategies for personal and professional success continues to challenge, inspire, and transform more achievers each year, as his audience continues to broaden to new arenas. Skip has served in the United States Marine Corps. He has stood in front and behind the camera, as the executive producer and host of his own self-help TV show called *The Skip Williams Sho*w. He is the creative author of *Think Progress*. He lives in New York City.